THE MONUMENTS OF

ANCIENT

EGYPT

THE MONUMENTS OF
ANCIENT
EGYPT

JEREMY STAFFORD-DEITSCH
FOREWORD BY T.G.H. JAMES

INDIANA UNIVERSITY PRESS
BLOOMINGTON AND INDIANAPOLIS

THIS BOOK WOULD NOT HAVE BEEN POSSIBLE WITHOUT THE BOUNDLESS HELP AND
GOODWILL OF NUMEROUS PEOPLE IN EGYPT. FIRST AND FOREMOST ARE THE GENERAL
DIRECTORS AT THE VARIOUS SITES WHO GRANTED ME PERMISSION TO PHOTOGRAPH.
IN PARTICULAR I WOULD LIKE TO THANK SABRY ABD EL AZIZ KHATER AND
MOHAMED EL BIALY AT LUXOR, AND ZAHI HAWASS AT GIZA.

First published in 2001
by The British Museum Press, a division of The British Museum Company Ltd, 46 Bloomsbury Street, London WC1B 3QQ

and in the United States
by Indiana University Press, 601 North Morton Street, Bloomington, IN 47404-3797
http://iupress.indiana.edu
1-800-842-6796

Cataloging information is available from the Library of Congress.
ISBN 0-253-34038-1 (cloth)
1 2 3 4 5 06 05 04 03 02 01

Designed by Molly Shields
Typeset in Garmond 3 and Poetica
Printed in Italy by Grafiche Milani

The illustrations in the Foreword were reproduced by kind permission of the following: pp. 8, 11 and 16 Jeremy Stafford-Deitsch;
pp. 9 and 13 T.G.H. James; p. 14 copyright The Griffith Institute, Ashmolean Museum, Oxford; pp. 18 and 19 The British Museum.

FRONTISPIECE The Great Sphinx at Giza is arguably the most famous and evocative of Egypt's monuments. Attributed to Khafra
(2558–2532 BC), it is illuminated by the rising sun and guards the approach to his pyramid.

CONTENTS

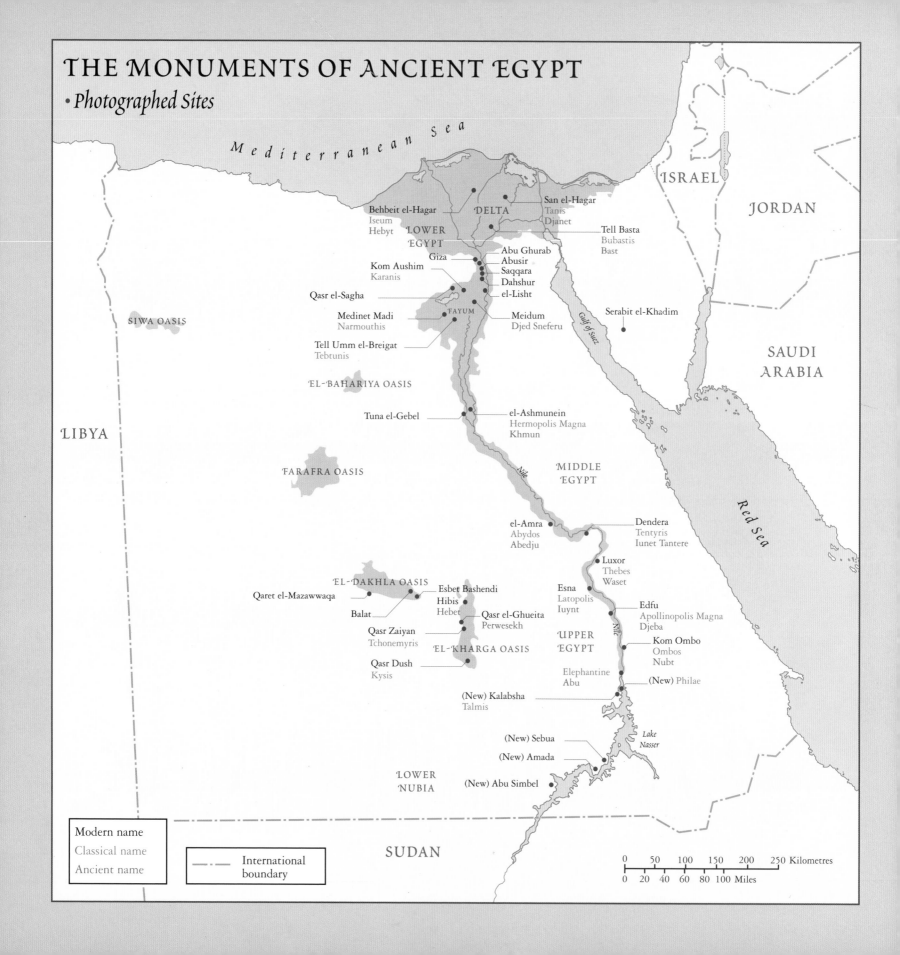

THE MONUMENTS OF ANCIENT EGYPT
• *Photographed Sites*

Mediterranean Sea

ISRAEL

JORDAN

DELTA

Behbeit el-Hagar
Iseum
Hebyt

San el-Hagar
Tanis
Djanet

LOWER
EGYPT

Tell Basta
Bubastis
Bast

Abu Ghurab
Giza
Abusir
Saqqara
Dahshur
el-Lisht

Kom Aushim
Karanis

Qasr el-Sagha

FAYUM

Meidum
Djed Sneferu

Serabit el-Khadim

Gulf of Suez

Medinet Madi
Narmouthis

Tell Umm el-Breigat
Tebtunis

SIWA OASIS

EL-BAHARIYA OASIS

LIBYA

Tuna el-Gebel

el-Ashmunein
Hermopolis Magna
Khmun

FARAFRA OASIS

Nile

MIDDLE
EGYPT

SAUDI
ARABIA

Red Sea

el-Amra
Abydos
Abedju

Dendera
Tentyris
Iunet Tantere

Luxor
Thebes
Waset

EL-DAKHLA OASIS

Qaret el-Mazawwaqa

Esbet Bashendi
Hibis
Hebet

Balat

Qasr Zaiyan
Tchonemyris

Qasr el-Ghueita
Perwesekh

EL-KHARGA OASIS

Qasr Dush
Kysis

Esna
Latopolis
Iuynt

Edfu
Apollinopolis Magna
Djeba

UPPER
EGYPT

Kom Ombo
Ombos
Nubt

Elephantine
Abu

Nile

(New) Philae

(New) Kalabsha
Talmis

*Lake
Nasser*

(New) Sebua

(New) Amada

LOWER
NUBIA

(New) Abu Simbel

SUDAN

0   50   100   150   200   250 Kilometres
0   20   40   60   80 100 Miles

FOREWORD: RECORDING THE ANCIENT MONUMENTS OF EGYPT

Few countries possess such spectacular monuments as Egypt; few countries arouse such extravagant feelings as Egypt. First-time visitors react as if they have made a personal discovery – which in a sense they have – and cannot wait to pass on their special, but by no means unique, reactions to others. In a letter written on New Year's Day 1850, Florence Nightingale, not quite thirty years old and before Crimea, expresses herself on Thebes like an excited school-girl:

> I could not believe that we should ever see Thebes; I was afraid to die, before our eyes should have lighted upon her. I had a dream the night before, that we had been obliged to turn back before we arrived.... Nothing can equal the first impression of seeing Thebes. We landed and ran up to Luxor, to see her temple before dark, her one obelisk still standing fresh, and unbroken as the day it was cut, before the propylaeum, at the gate of which sit two colossi of Rameses II.

The written word provided Florence Nightingale with her preferred method of recording and purveying information and impressions. Her descriptions of monuments are enthusiastic and fair, but based on little knowledge of the country, and with only the slightest acquaintance with the hieroglyphic script. It was, after all, scarcely a quarter of a century since Champollion made his great announcement on decipherment to the Académie des inscriptions et belles-lettres, and there were few books of a general kind about Egypt and its monuments to which Florence Nightingale and her travelling companions, Charles and Selina Bracebridge, could turn for information and guidance. They had, however, done some preparation, and travelled with a small library of useful books, including apparently Sir John Gardner Wilkinson's *Manners and Customs of the Ancient Egyptians* and his immensely practical *Modern Egypt and Thebes* in two volumes, the first useful guidebook for travellers in Egypt. They knew of, and probably had with them, G.-B. Belzoni's *Narrative* and the first volumes of Baron Bunsen's *Egypt's Place in Universal History*, recently translated into English from the original German. Florence Nightingale had called on Bunsen in London, where he was Prussian Ambassador, and had, it seems, acquired the best up-to-date information for her journey to Egypt. Her letters also make reference to the works of Champollion and Lepsius, of James Bruce who travelled to Egypt and Abyssinia in the later 18th century, and David Roberts, whose splendidly evocative lithographs of Egypt, Nubia, and other Eastern Mediterranean lands, had only recently been published.

A brilliant pen can always invoke a place, investing it with the magical perception of the gifted writer. Wilkinson wrote superbly, and his work with pencil and paint-brush was not without merit; Belzoni's *Narrative* is lively and informative, but his own painted illustrations scarcely do justice to his discoveries. Neither Wilkinson nor Belzoni could compete graphically with David Roberts, a well-trained and experienced artist by the time he travelled to Egypt in 1838–9. For many he remains the artist of Egyptian monuments whose work represents all one would wish to remember of those magical places. His paintings have been pillaged to illustrate so many books on Egypt; his plates have been stripped from their bound volumes to grace the walls of Egyptian hotels and of private drawing rooms everywhere. But the curious student of ancient Egypt can learn far more about the details of monuments and of the culture of the ancient land from the drawings and

The hypostyle hall at Karnak by David Roberts, from EGYPT AND NUBIA,
*1846–50. At this time the temple had not yet been cleared of the rubble of millennia,
or suffered the earthquake that toppled the columns later in the 19th century.*

with good equipment, a good eye, and a knowledgeable approach. Even the amateur photographer cannot fail on occasion to capture the essence of Egypt with his lens. Almost everyone with any artistic ability feels obliged to resort to drawing pad, to pencil, pen or brush when faced by the reality of Egypt. The desire to record is compelling, and the visual quality of the country and its monuments demands to be captured in one way or another. Recording, however, may be casual, but it can also be severely intended, and the history of the recording of Egypt with serious intent is long and distinguished. From the middle of the 18th century, when access to Egypt became less hazardous than in earlier times, serious attempts were made to present the literate public with books which set out not only to describe the monuments of the country, but to present images of them as well. In some cases the traveller-authors looked beyond the simple presentation of images, understanding that there was the need to copy the scenes and inscriptions, so lavishly inscribed on the monuments, as carefully as possible, in the expectation – vain as it must have seemed at the time – that in due course hieroglyphics would yield up their secrets and tell the story of a lost antiquity.

The most important and influential work of this kind during the 18th century was Norden's *Travels in Egypt and Nubia*, originally published in French in 1755 and then in English in 1757. Frederik Ludwig Norden was a Danish naval officer who was sent to Egypt in 1738 by King Christian VI to make a survey of the country and its monuments. He travelled south up the Nile, beyond the First Cataract at Aswan, but not as far as Abu Simbel. He drew the countryside and the monuments wherever he went, and in due course his drawings were used as the basis for engravings which illustrated his two volumes. He spent his last years in London and was elected a Fellow of the Royal Society in 1740. Sadly, he died in 1742, and his volumes were prepared for publication posthumously with plates engraved without his knowledgeable supervision. The published results were travesties of his original drawings, which fortunately, are preserved safely in

watercolours of Wilkinson and Belzoni than from the finished lithographs of David Roberts. To say so is not to diminish Roberts's achievement, but to distinguish it from that of the former two, who may properly be included in the list of pioneer Egyptologists.

The landscape, the light and the monuments of Egypt bring out the best in the photographer and the artist. The plates in this volume – the work of a very skilled practitioner – demonstrate what can be achieved

Copenhagen. Nevertheless, the two volumes were remarkably successful and were frequently reprinted.

Norden's *Travels* was a pioneer work which by its text informed with fair accuracy the interested reader, and by its plates offered tantalizing views, more numerous and comprehensive than any previously published, of the enigmatic monuments of Egypt. Norden's efforts to be accurate may have in the result been somewhat frustrated, but the stimulation of interest aroused was of lasting importance. Unfortunately, those who were stimulated, and might have been able to indulge their interest by travelling to Egypt, were denied the opportunity until the early years of the 19th century.

Egypt did not become part of the Grand Tour until after the collapse of the French expedition to Egypt under Napoleon in 1801, and the subsequent opening-up of the country under the regime of Muhammed Ali Pasha. But the stimulus for the recording and study of the monuments was provided by the French expedition. Napoleon included in his entourage a group of *savants*, scholars of many disciplines, who were charged to examine and make note of all aspects of Egypt as they found it: geography, geology, natural history, social customs, history and, above all, antiquities. An Institut established in Cairo provided a base for these learned men, and a depot to

An imaginative painting by an unidentified artist of about 1800, containing elements of several mortuary temples in Western Thebes, artistically repositioned. The artist probably drew his inspiration from the engravings by Norden.

which could be sent specimens, including sculptures and other ancient objects.

Among the last was the Rosetta Stone with its three bands of text (two Egyptian and one Greek), discovered by chance in 1799 by Pierre François Xavier Bouchard, an officer in charge of fortification works at Rashid (Rosetta) on the coast some miles to the northeast of Alexandria. From the moment of its discovery it was recognized as offering the possibility of the decipherment of the ancient Egyptian scripts, a possibility which had previously seemed unattainable even by scholars who had devoted many years to the study of hieroglyphics. It would be over twenty years before the crucial breakthrough would be made by Jean François Champollion, but during the intervening years the chances for decipherment became increasingly strong, and the real need to record accurately scenes and inscriptions became increasingly appreciated. The process had begun during the French occupation. Artists of the Commission, working with the scholars of the Institut, made copies of many of the visible scenes and inscriptions on the standing monuments, and these would be published in due course in the massive folios of the *Description de l'Égypte*.

Among the artists was Dominique Vivant Denon, an upper-class Frenchman who managed to escape the terrors of the revolutionary agents, and travelled to Egypt with the Napoleonic expedition, although apparently not as an official member of the Commission. Many of the drawings he made were included in the *Description*, but many were reserved for his own personal publication, *Voyage dans la Basse et la Haute Égypte* (1802). The English translation, *Travels in Upper and Lower Egypt*, appeared in 1803 and soon became an essential part of the baggage of early 19th-century travellers to Egypt. The illustrations were good, mostly showing general views of places and well-known monuments; it was an appetite-whetter rather than a scholarly work, but first in the field of illustrated travel books, post-Napoleon and anticipating the more serious publications of those who drew and copied with the prospect of hieroglyphic decipherment in mind.

The great volumes of the *Description de l'Égypte* began to be issued in 1809, five volumes of plates being devoted to antiquities. It was the first attempt at a comprehensive coverage of Egyptian monuments from the Delta to Aswan. It incorporated much of Denon's work, but the majority of the plates were based on the drawings and paintings of the regular artists of the Napoleonic Commission, chief of whom was Prosper Jollois, who had a part in preparing the ultimate publication. The official artists had lacked Denon's freedom of movement, and worked under direction throughout the Nile Valley, spending many days at each site of importance and producing ostensibly careful copies of what was visible on the walls of tombs, temples and other standing monuments. The published results, unsupervised in the plate-making – as had been the case with Norden's work – were not nearly as accurate as they appeared to be superficially. In 1818 Henry Salt, Consul-General of Great Britain in Egypt, a well-trained artist and devoted student of hieroglyphics, writing to Lord Mountnorris, a former patron, criticized in detail the plates of the *Description* devoted to the royal tombs in the Valley of the Kings: 'Everything they have done from the Kings' Tombs, which is all I have yet closely compared, is exceedingly bad, especially in what belongs to the colours, which are most perversely contrary to those in the originals.' H.H. Halls, who edited Salt's letters, expresses some surprise at Salt's strictures. He had himself inspected in Paris the drawings of Du Tertre, one of the Commission's artists: 'I confess I have never seen anything in water-colours that surpassed his productions, either in the beauty of their execution or in the strong internal evidence they bore of the most scrupulous accuracy.' He adds that he believed Salt himself held a similar opinion of Du Tertre's work, and he surmises that this artist might 'have had little to do with the superintendance of the *publication* of the great French work'. These comments show how soon in the 19th century the pioneers of Egyptology were beginning to appreciate the importance of accuracy in the copying of the scenes and inscriptions of ancient Egypt, and in their printing.

View of the Temple of Isis at Philae from the DESCRIPTION DE L'ÉGYPTE. *Before the temple was flooded annually after the construction of the first Aswan Dam, its reliefs were notable for the presence of much original colour.*

The early students of decipherment, labouring away in their studies – Champollion in Grenoble, Thomas Young in London – were hampered by the paucity of available texts to work on. There was the Rosetta Stone, a few published copies of texts and the drawn copies sent to them by helpful workers in Egypt. The last were inevitably of uncertain accuracy; no one knew what might be significant in detail in the form of a sign; no one could determine the date of a text, although it was known that Egyptian history spanned several thousand years. The smallest variation might mean something. So accuracy had to be a paramount concern, and accuracy could only be achieved by care and by the exercise of the eye and the skill of good artists. In this crucial period, when the certainty of decipherment became increasingly sure, it was fortunate that there were adventurous travellers with scholarly instincts who were prepared to spend long periods of time – many years in some cases – copying and organizing the copying, of monumental texts. In most cases they were confident that they were not only contributing to the advance of understanding of ancient Egyptian writing, but also recording what might not survive in the future. Between 1815 and 1835 in particular, heroic work was accomplished, and even if the results of the copyists were not always published, their careful work has been preserved for posterity, with in many cases better copies than can ever now be achieved because of the wilful destruction of vandals and unthinking people, and the ravages of time.

Of the independent copyists, one of the first was William John Bankes, scion of a landed family in Dorset, who made two extended journeys up the Nile in 1815 and 1818–19, accompanied by professional artists, and copying all the way. His dragoman and right-hand man was Giovanni-Battista Finati, who noted on the first voyage, 'We were landing almost continually, wherever there were tidings or expectation of any vestige of antiquity, and I soon grew so accustomed to see Mr Bankes drawing and noting from them, that I began to take some interest in the sight of them myself.' Bankes had no special training for this work, and absolutely no need to endure the difficulties of working in harsh conditions. His interest had been stimulated by the scholarly enthusiasm of Jean-Louis Burckhardt, a Swiss orientalist working in the Near East for the Association for Promoting the Discovery of the Interior Parts of Africa; and this interest survived the tragically early death of Burckhardt in 1817. Bankes's second Nile journey became altogether a much more organised campaign in which he was joined by Henry Salt, only recently appointed British Consul-General in Egypt.

Salt had been recommended to Bankes by Burckhardt. He had thrown himself enthusiastically into the recording of monuments after his arrival in Egypt, possibly also at the urging of Burckhardt, who recognized Salt's artistic talent. In a letter to Bankes, then travelling in Syria, Burckhardt reported: 'Mr Salt is eagerly occupied in collecting and drawing Hieroglyphics, of which we have never had any correct design till now. In pursuing this plan he will do more towards their explication than has ever been done before.' When Salt joined Bankes in the autumn of 1818 their expedition contained three further artists, one of whom, Louis Linant de Bellefonds, was unusually talented, an excellent watercolourist as well as draughtsman. All together there were five artists of varying abilities who developed a kind of rivalry between themselves which contributed substantially to the amount of drawing they achieved. Salt commented in a letter to a friend, 'All . . . were enthusiastically fond of the arts, and really vied with each other who should produce the best sketches; being generally occupied *hard at it*. . . from nine o'clock in the morning till dark.' Their industry reached a peak of intensity at Abu Simbel, where the great rock-temple of King Ramesses II had only recently been opened by Belzoni at Salt's expense. The party spent a month working inside the temple, copying for the first time the bulk of the scenes and inscriptions carved on the walls. They had no plans for publication, but a record was made which remains of value to the present day.

After William Bankes's return to Britain in the summer of 1819, Henry Salt remained in Cairo. There he continued his work of recording on a reduced scale, and involved himself increasingly in the debate over decipherment, engaging in controversy with others over matters of detail and interpretation, his position in Egypt itself investing his opinions with particular validity. But he remained a point of contact and an invaluable support for British proto-Egyptologists until his premature death in 1827.

John Gardner Wilkinson, who came to Egypt in 1821, was initially taken under Salt's wing in Cairo, but subsequently settled in Thebes, working independently and with great scholarly profit until 1833 without once leaving the country. He undertook a huge amount of copying, particularly in the private tombs at Thebes and elsewhere in the Nile Valley, and he wrote some of the very first systematic and well-informed books on Egypt and its ancient culture. His *Manners and Customs* (1837) remained useful until well into the 20th century, especially in its revision by Samuel Birch of The British Museum in 1878, and is still consulted for the numerous drawings of Egyptian life, occupations and social activities, based on Wilkinson's studies on the ground. As already mentioned, it was one of the books on which Florence Nightingale relied during her Nile voyage.

Copies of the painted reliefs of two harpists in the tomb of King Ramesses III (c. 1184–1153 BC) in the Valley of the Kings, by John Gardner Wilkinson.

Wilkinson's house at Thebes, in which he incorporated a spacious but much damaged tomb-chapel, enlarged with mud-brick extensions and towers, became a regular point of call for visitors who were engaged on work on the monuments. It was on occasion almost a club where like-minded students of antiquity were made welcome in very congenial surroundings. It became even more so when it was occupied by Robert Hay after Wilkinson's departure from Thebes in 1832. One of Hay's fellow copyists, George Alexander Hoskins, describes how

On Thursday evenings . . . the artists and travellers at Thebes used to assemble at his house, or rather tomb I should call it; but never was the habitation of death witness to gayer scenes. Though we wore the costume, we did not always preserve the gravity of Turks; and the saloon, although formerly a sepulchre, threw no gloom over our mirth. We were all fond of the arts, and had proved our devotion to antiquarian pursuits by sacrificing for a time Europe and its enjoyments, to prosecute our researches in a distant land. Our conversation therefore never flagged; and assuredly I reckon, not among the least happy hours of my life, the evenings spent in the tomb at Thebes.

Robert Hay, with the artists and colleagues who worked with him, established almost an industry of copying which they engaged in throughout the country and in the oases in the Western Desert. The results of their labours are preserved in forty-nine bound volumes in the British Library, a treasure-trove of exact and beautiful drawings and watercolours scarcely used in Hay's lifetime for publication, but remaining a rich source of reference for scholars to this day. Hay's purpose, as with earlier copyists, was to record, and not necessarily to publish. At the time there was still much debate over the certainty of Champollion's decipherment. Wilkinson was a Champollion man. It is not certain whether Hay had a view one way or the other. Hoskins had much uncertainty, but believed greatly in the value of copying. Writing of copies he made in the temple of Darius I in el-Kharga Oasis where he was working with Hay in 1832, he declared:

Could tablets of hieroglyphics be deciphered with the same facility as Greek and Latin inscriptions, I would publish the copy which I make of this tablet, since it is scarcely probable that so long an inscription can be destitute of information. If the mists and darkness which impede hieroglyphical research shall ever be cleared away, and if the light of science shall ever penetrate all this mystery of antiquarian lore, what extraordinary and interesting relations may perhaps be unfolded to us; and what perplexing mythological and metaphysical subtleties be elucidated!

While many of the copyists working in Egypt in the early decades of the 19th century relied almost entirely on their simple skills as artists to make their copies, some found it convenient to use particular aids to help them in dealing with difficult, especially large, subjects. An optical device used by Hay and his best assistant, Joseph Bonomi, and other competent copyists like George Hoskins and Edward William Lane, was the camera lucida. It was by no means a camera in the now accepted sense, but a very simple, easily portable, piece of equipment incorporating a prism, replaceable in various sizes, by which an image of what was to be drawn could be viewed on a sheet of paper and drawn with all the main features accurately juxtaposed. It was a convenient tool best used for laying out speedily the general features of a scene or view, for placing a monument in a landscape.

Some copyists made use of squeezes to secure a permanent mechanical record of a scene or text cut in

Drawing of the Armant temple of Montu, south of Thebes, by George Alexander Hoskins. The considerable remains shown here were dismantled in the mid-19th century and much of the stone used for the building of a sugar factory.

relief, especially as they could train their Egyptian workmen to take the squeezes. The process consisted in making impressions or casts in suitable paper – a 'stiff, unsized, common white paper', as Hoskins described it. The paper was dampened and placed, damp side outwards, on the area to be squeezed, then pressed with a stiff brush, a bunched cloth or even the fingers, over the carved surface, securing in this way an impression which would be firm and quite durable when dry. It is not a process to be recommended now. Wilkinson used it on painted reliefs, apparently with the wet side against the carved surface, so that his squeezes brought away with them much of any surviving colour. The method was also used by the technicians on the great Prussian expedition to be mentioned shortly, but with great care and less loss of colour. Many years later Howard Carter, in his early days in Egypt, when he was employed principally as an artist, experimented with dry squeezes, but found the method too laborious and slow. He preferred to rely on his eye, as did Robert Hay, whose work Carter particularly admired.

During the time when Hay and his team, and others, were busy in Luxor and elsewhere, a large, well-organized epigraphic enterprise was in the field under the supervision of Jean François Champollion. His French *équipe* was supplemented by an almost equally large Italian party led by Ippolito Rosellini. This Franco-Tuscan officially sponsored expedition repeated to some extent the work of the Napoleonic Commission, but under more settled circumstances, and with the knowledge that what was being copied was already capable of being partially understood. Champollion's presence gave the undertaking great prestige; his linguistic discoveries were already well known, and their results being tested by the more scholarly copyists like Wilkinson. The expedition worked steadily in 1828 and 1829, and much of the material, especially the copies of Nestor l'Hôte, an exceptionally gifted draughtsman and artist, was of a very high standard. While they worked at Thebes there were opportunities for social exchanges between the French and the British 'amateurs', who were unfairly,

but understandably, critical of the Franco-Tuscan work. James Burton, one of the most prodigious of the British copyists, discussing the figures in many of the plates produced by the opposition, found 'some too lanky, some too fat, some too muscular'. The subsequent publications in huge folios, *Monumenti dell'Egitto e della Nubia* (1832–44) and *Monuments de l'Égypte et de la Nubie* (1835–45), appeared after Champollion's death (1832), and were therefore denied any supervision in their production by the master himself. Rosellini died before the completion of the publications (1843). There is much duplication between the French and the Italian series, and they both suffer from the inadequate techniques and lack of control employed in the conversion of excellent drawings into indifferent plates. Nevertheless, both monumental series made a huge amount of material available for study by scholars who were unable to travel to Egypt and see the monuments themselves.

The heroic age of amateur enterprise in the copying of Egyptian monuments came to a gradual end during the 1830s. It never utterly died because serious students of the monuments and of the texts and scenes they carry remained persuaded to believe that nothing printed could be wholly relied on, and that personal inspection and copying were essential for proper scholarly study. As knowledge of hieroglyphics and of the intricacies of the Egyptian language developed, accuracy in copies was increasingly required, and the development of epigraphic skills was pursued professionally from the later 19th century by institutions like the Egypt Exploration Fund (now Society) and the French Institute in Cairo. The process continues today, with the institutionalized co-operation of artists and scholars. And yet, even now when a text is to be carefully studied, few Egyptologists with strict standards of accuracy will meekly accept what may be already published, even in works prepared, and supervised in their printing, by colleagues with equally strict standards. It was A.E. Housman, a precise classical scholar, who reckoned that accuracy in publication was a duty, not a virtue.

Accuracy, as well as comprehensiveness, was one of

Copy of a war relief of Ramesses II in the Ramesseum from Émile Prisse d'Avennes' HISTOIRE DE L'ART ÉGYPTIEN D'APRÈS LES MONUMENTS *(1878),*
one of the last of the massive folio works on Egypt.

the primary aims of Richard Lepsius, who organized and led the last great expedition to Egypt to carry out a survey comparable with those of the Napoleonic Commission and the Franco-Tuscan enterprise. Lepsius was a well-trained German Egyptologist – one of the first of a new and distinctive breed – who persuaded the King of Prussia to sponsor the expedition. It would not only record the ancient monuments of Egypt and Nubia, but also undertake excavation and the acquisi-

tion of antiquities for the Berlin Museum. He gathered a team of skilled artists, including Joseph Bonomi who had worked with Robert Hay, surveyors, craftsmen and supporting staff. From 1842 to 1845 they quartered the country, taking with great care many thousands of squeezes of texts, plaster casts of reliefs, and a vast quantity of drawings. The ensuing publication, *Denkmäler aus Aegypten und Aethiopien* in twelve massive volumes (1849–59), was the ultimate production in the elephantine mode which had prevailed for almost fifty years. Unlike its predecessors, however, it was almost wholly trustworthy. Under Lepsius's guidance a very superior result was achieved, and, although the diligent scholar may detect weaknesses and inaccuracies, its reliability as a work of reference is to this day greatly admired.

Careful copying with the co-operation of artists and scholars continues up to the present day as the most acceptable and reliable method of recording an Egyptian monument for scientific publication. The procedures used in copying vary according to tradition and particular practice, but the aim in most cases is to produce drawings of scenes and texts which can be reduced in size for reproduction as plates in a volume. Some expeditions use direct tracing as the principal method, others use a combination of photography and drawing. No one now draws directly from wall to paper as the early copyists did. Howard Carter believed that direct drawing in pencil was the surest way of securing accurate *and artistic* results, and the products of his skills were recognized and admired long before he became famous for the discovery of the tomb of Tutankhamun. But he was a superlatively good draughtsman with a wonderful eye and a well-trained hand. In all cases of modern copying the knowledge and skill of the epigrapher – the term used for one who copies and studies inscriptions – are essential for the accuracy of the final result. Knowledge and skill are especially important when an inscribed wall is badly damaged, or when a text has been changed or partly obliterated in antiquity; a final result may require many hours spent at the wall, in different lights and corresponding shadows, at night with a lamp as well as by day. No photograph can achieve what the human eye can make out by persistence. Nevertheless, photography has an important place in the epigraphic processes, and it is now essential in the general recording of monuments. Even if it cannot seriously compete in the recording of minutiae with the methods of the old-fashioned copyist, photography's mechanical aspect renders it of particular value.

Photography in Egypt has an illustrious history.

William Henry Fox Talbot, the inventor of the calotype, also called talbotype, a process by which a negative was produced from which multiple copies could be made, never himself practised in Egypt. It was, however, used there with success by other practitioners such as John Shaw Smith, who took several hundred calotypes on a visit to the Near East and Egypt from 1850 to 1852. Fox Talbot did use the method to photograph archaeological subjects, including Egyptian inscriptions and cuneiform texts. The potential value of photography was quickly appreciated, especially as techniques improved. Among the first to use regular photography in Egypt was Maxime du Camp, who travelled in the Eastern Mediterranean with Gustave Flaubert in 1849–50, and published a volume, *Égypte, Nubie, Palestine et Syrie* (1852) illustrated with his photographs – one of the first such books ever published.

The first person seriously to commercialize the photographic possibilities of Egypt was Francis Frith, who made several visits to Egypt, the first being in 1856. His photographs of Egyptian scenes and monuments were of an extraordinary quality; he used a large-scale camera, capable of taking plates of 20 × 16 in (50.8 × 40.6 cm). He also used a stereo camera with which he produced a stereo series which became especially popular. Working with wet glass plates in conditions which were far from ideal – heat, wind-blown sand, swarms of tiny flies, persistent, curious locals – and developing results in a travelling dark-room, made photographic expeditions unusually trying. But the known results are among the best ever achieved by photography in Egypt. Mid-19th-century photographs are mostly of landscape and monuments in landscape of a general kind; there are occasional shots of especially striking scenes and texts on monuments. These early photographs are very valuable in showing monuments as they were before they were freed from the accumulations of millennia of rubble and rubbish, and before they were subjected to mindless vandalism, some of it sadly the result of uncontrolled clearance by the embryonic Antiquities Service.

In the publication of volumes aimed at a general

Abu Simbel from EGYPT AND PALESTINE *vol. I by Francis Frith (1858–60). At the time of Frith's visit, the façade of the temple was still encumbered by mounds of drift-sand.*

The sculptured gateway at Karnak from EGYPT AND PALESTINE *vol. I by Francis Frith (1858–60): the propylon built in front of the temple of Khonsu by King Ptolemy III Euergetes I (246–222 BC).*

audience, the tradition of Norden and Denon, and later of David Roberts, was refreshed by the new technology of photography. The tradition continued throughout the second half of the 19th century and the whole of the 20th century. Colour photography has greatly increased the possibility of conveying the vibrancy and dramatic effect of Egyptian monuments in a spectacular environment. The present volume, in which the practices of Francis Frith have in a sense been revived in modern terms, especially in the use of a large format camera, demonstrates the extent to which sensitive, ungimmicky, photography may present Egyptian monuments in their natural settings in a most admirable way. There is something immensely satisfying in this series of photographs; above all, it preserves a record of the chosen monuments as they are at the beginning of the 21st century, which will remain of permanent value. Egypt is not immune from the effects of modern life, and we cannot expect that what can be seen in these splendid photographs will remain in an immutable state for ever, as the ancient Egyptians themselves might have piously hoped.

T.G.H. James

INTRODUCTION

Photography is not what it was. The almost total victory of the 35 mm camera – its effortless, instantaneous, high-quality snapshots – and the growing challenge of the digital photography of the computer age, make the painstaking processes of the past seem obsolete.

One hundred and fifty years ago cameras were bulky and awkward to use. A tripod was essential. There was something comically heroic about the Victorian travel photographer dragging his Heath Robinson contraptions – including home-made portable darkroom – from site to site. A shutter speed of many seconds was inevitably required by the combination of insensitive (or 'slow') photographic image-making process and the small lens aperture necessary for adequate depth of field. This meant that anything moving ended up blurred in the photograph. In 1849, when Maxime du Camp photographed his Nubian servant astride a colossus at Abu Simbel, he solved this problem by informing his servant that the camera was a gun and that if he moved he would be shot. The photograph is splendid – even if the tactics are dubious.

The great Egyptian sites were then a mixture of the standing and fallen, the tilting and the collapsed with much still submerged by desert sand and Nile sediment. One of the greatest of the early photographers, Francis Frith (1822–98), approached the photographing of Karnak's hypostyle hall with trepidation because he doubted whether he could do justice to the vast combination of the chaotic and the monumental. Nowadays, with so many of the sites restored, something evocative has vanished though other photographic possibilities have occasionally emerged.

The design of the modern large-format 'view camera' is little changed from that of Victorian times. A view camera was used for the images in this book.

A sheet of film is required for each photograph (the standard modern size is 4 × 5 inches). This means that the tiniest details can be recorded. A wall of hieroglyphs retains its intricacies even when the large-format photograph is enlarged considerably. The other great advantage of this type of camera is the ability to move the lens relative to the position of the film plane. For example, when photographing tall columns close up from ground level, a camera with a fixed lens will invariably have to be tilted upwards to fit in all of the subject. This will result in the unpleasant and unnatural effect of converging verticals: in the photograph the columns look as if they are leaning in towards each other. With the view camera, the lens itself can be moved independent of the film plane. By raising (or 'shifting') the lens itself upwards (rather than tilting the whole camera) the perspective is maintained and the columns remain parallel in the photograph.

The totalitarian certainties that the pyramids sought to express can be glimpsed in a photograph. The majority of the other monuments lack viewpoints from where their details intentionally 'click'. They require no audience. To look at this architecture is to remember the philosophical question of what something looks like when no one is looking at it. The purpose, such as it was, was processional rather than static and the insistence that space, grandiosity, order and light must lead into the claustrophobic, into the cramped and stuffy heat of secret darkness, reverses the basic 'outlook' of the western rational tradition. The architects were addressing the raw fundamentals of superstition and our first spellbound responses – amazement and awe – are soon jolted by the barbarity (Ramesses III depicted on the walls of his mortuary temple piles of the severed hands and phalluses of his enemies).

We are haunted by these monuments because they are the evocative interface with everything that we thought we had left behind. If these photographs remind visitors of their own unexpected impressions, or galvanize others into wanting to visit these gloriously naive yet devastatingly numinous attempts to cast the human condition in a very different light, they will have served a purpose.

View across from the Old Cataract Hotel at Aswan to the southern tip of Elephantine Island. The ruins are of the once fortified town that guarded the border. In the foreground is the balcony favoured by King Farouk (AD 1936–1952), Egypt's last king (if the one-year reign of his infant son is discounted). On the horizon, in the centre, is the mausoleum of Aga Khan III (AD 1877–1957). To its right is the ancient monastery of Saint Simeon.

THE DELTA

The ancient Egyptians thought of their country as divided into two parts. To the south, upstream, was the desert-fringed ribbon of fertility of Upper Egypt. This stretched from one of the various Nubian cataracts (the border changed according to political circumstance) to the ancient and strategically placed capital of Memphis. To the north of this, downstream, was the very different landscape of Lower Egypt: the broad, flat, fertile, swampy land of the Delta.

Upper and Lower Egypt had their own specific goddesses: the vulture goddess Nekhbet from ancient Nekheb (el-Kab, 70 kilometres south of Luxor) for the former and the cobra goddess Wadjet from Buto in the north-western Delta for the latter. These two goddesses appear at the beginning of the so-called 'Two Ladies' or *nebty* name of the pharaoh. Likewise, when each successive pharaoh ascended the throne he took the title 'Lord of the Two Lands' signifying that he had unified the country. This reflected the culmination of a prehistoric process of probably first cultural and then political unification which was completed in about 3000 BC.

Annual silt deposition from the Nile (prior to the building of the High Dam in the 1960s) has caused the major part of the archaeological material of the Delta to be buried, while agricultural practices, rebuilding and human expansion have all taken a heavy toll.

Historically the Delta's prime significance derived from its proximity to the Levantine and Mediterranean worlds. The Hyksos, who infiltrated from Palestine during the Middle Kingdom (2055–1650 BC) and ruled Lower Egypt during the latter part of the Second Intermediate Period (1650–1550 BC), had their capital at Avaris (modern Tell el-Daba) in the eastern Delta.

During their sojourn in Lower Egypt they appear to have looked to Palestine for the majority of their needs while trading and negotiating with the other regions of Egypt on a mostly peaceful basis.

At the height of the New Kingdom Ramesses II (1279–1213 BC) founded a splendid new capital, Piramesse (modern Qantir), near to the ancient Hyksos capital. It was probably from this area that the family had originated and where Ramesses II's father, Seti I, had built a summer palace. Sadly little now remains of Piramesse.

During the Third Intermediate Period (1069–747 BC) the rulers of the 21st and 22nd Dynasties transported many of the statues, obelisks and columns of Piramesse to their nearby capital of Tanis (San el-Hagar) where they enrich what is now the most impressive archaeological site in the Delta. In 1939 the royal burials were discovered at Tanis – a discovery as significant as that of the tomb of Tutankhamun in the Valley of the Kings in 1922, but less publicized at the time because of the outbreak of the Second World War.

During the Graeco-Roman Period (332 BC–AD 395), Egypt looked ever more towards the Classical world and the Delta was developed accordingly. The modern city of Alexandria has obliterated the city founded by Alexander the Great in 332 BC – a city that became the most culturally diverse, wealthy and architecturally spectacular in the Classical world.

In 1799 French soldiers at Rosetta (el-Rashid) in the western Delta discovered the famous Rosetta Stone now in The British Museum. Recording a decree of Ptolemy V Epiphanes (205–180 BC) in Greek, demotic (a cursive script) and hieroglyphs, it provided the key for the decipherment of Egyptian demotic and hieroglyphs by Thomas Young and Jean-François Champollion respectively.

This statue, at San el-Hagar (classical name: Tanis), portrays an idealized New Kingdom pharaoh (probably Ramesses II, 1279–1213 BC) in traditional form: he wears the NEMES headcloth, the false beard and the URAEUS which represents the protective cobra goddess The Great Enchantress.

BELOW AND OPPOSITE *The temple of Isis at Behebeit el-Hagar (classical name: Iseum) was built by Nectanebo II (360–343 BC); the superb relief decorations date to Ptolemy II Philadelphus (285–246 BC). This was a major cult centre for Isis. The fact that a block from this temple was reused in a temple in Rome renovated by Domitian (AD 81–96) suggests that it had already collapsed by then.*

BELOW *San el-Hagar (classical name: Tanis) is the most imposing ancient site in the Delta. Although most of its construction dates to the 21st and 22nd Dynasties (1069–715 BC), the majority of the obelisks, columns and statues are derived from Piramesse, the plundered capital of Ramesses II (1279–1213 BC).*

OPPOSITE *Herodotus visited Tell Basta (classical name: Bubastis), the cult centre of the lioness/cat goddess Bastet, in the late 5th century BC and described its temple as the loveliest in Egypt. Little now remains. This relief of Bastet in lioness form extrudes from an archaeological trench.*

SINAI

The Egyptians of the Nile Valley required, from the earliest times, metals and precious stones from farther afield. They considered the precious materials of neighbouring deserts to be theirs by right; it was a right that could at times require considerable logistical support to be enforced. Desert nomads were often a threat and so mining expeditions beyond the Nile Valley tended to occur during periods of ambitious political expansion and subsequent stability: a Middle Kingdom rock inscription from quarries in the Wadi Hammamat (in the desert east of Qift, Upper Egypt) states that 3000 troops were at hand, their presence having been facilitated by the subjugation of the local tribes by an advance guard.

In the desert west of the Nile Valley lived a tribe that the Egyptians called the Libu, from which the modern name Libya presumably derives. Caravan routes that incorporated the oases ran through this region but the desert itself was not significant for mining. The eastern desert was not fully exploited until the Roman occupation (30 BC–AD 395). In it were to be found amethyst and beryl as well as a variety of semi-precious stones. It also yielded metals – copper, tin, gold – and numerous prized stones such as graywacke, basalt, diorite and marble. The Roman mines of Mons Claudianus and Mons Porphyrites were used exclusively to supply granite and porphyry for imperial monuments: columns in the Pantheon in Rome, for example, originated from Mons Claudianus.

In the eastern Sinai, 30 kilometres north of modern Eilat, were the ancient copper mines of Timna. Egyptian expeditions worked them as early as the New Kingdom with the co-operation of Midianites and the local Amalekites. It was here that the Egyptians produced some of the earliest known ventilated, multi-layered and complex mines. Hathor, the cow-headed goddess, was the protectress of miners; a temple dedicated to her was built by Seti I (1294–1279 BC) at Timna which has yielded numerous votive remains.

The western Sinai was mined for its turquoise from the earliest historical times. The main sites were Wadi Maghara and Serabit el-Khadim, the latter remaining in operation until the late New Kingdom: Ramesses VI (1143–1136 BC) is the last attested presence. The core of this site is of considerable archaeological interest because it is a rare example of a Middle Kingdom temple. A Shrine of Kings commemorated via statuary the ruler who had ordered the latest expedition while also honouring his predecessors. The expedition leader, as the king's representative, was also portrayed.

The prime rock-cut temple (or *speos*) at Serabit el-Khadim was dedicated to Hathor 'lady of the turquoise'. A Middle Kingdom sanctuary to the Memphite god Ptah next to it was replaced in the early New Kingdom by a *speos* to Hathor, Amun of Thebes and the desert god Soped. A processional route lined with chapels leads to the sanctuaries. There are numerous stelae scattered through the ruins whose eroded texts throw light on the mining expeditions as well as the religious practices at the site. Serabit el-Khadim, perched on its flat-topped mountain, is nowadays a dilapidated site in a spectacular setting. Inscriptions by the Egyptians based at the temple can also be seen on the rock faces of the precipitous mountain path that leads to the temple.

The temple at Serabit el-Khadim was primarily dedicated to the cow-goddess Hathor who was, amongst her many roles, patroness of miners. She could be portrayed on the capitals of columns with the face or just the ears of a cow. To the right is a stela erected by one of the expedition leaders.

On the right of a New Kingdom block at Serabit el-Khadim, Hatshepsut (1473–1458 BC) offers to a composite god consisting of the divine huntsman Onuris and the sky god Shu. On the left, her co-regent Tuthmosis III can be discerned offering to Hathor.

View along the processional route towards the Middle Kingdom rock-cut sanctuary of Hathor at Serabit el-Khadim. On the stela in the left foreground,
Tuthmosis III (1479–1425 BC) and his expedition leader Ty offer to Hathor. The last line of hieroglyphs reads 'Beloved of Hathor, lady of turquoise'.

GIZA

The Giza pyramids were built by three rulers of the 4th Dynasty: Khufu (or Cheops) (2589–2566 BC), builder of the Great Pyramid; his son Khafra (Chephren) (2558–2532 BC), builder of the Second Pyramid and the Great Sphinx; and thirdly Menkaura (Mycerinus) (2532–2503 BC), son of Khafra and builder of the Third Pyramid.

To the ancient Egyptians, life was associated with dawn and the east, while death was associated with dusk and the west: thus the tendency throughout Egyptian history for tombs to be located on the west bank of the Nile. A valley temple, accessible to the Nile via a canal and possibly fronted by a harbour, was the disembarkation point of the deceased king's river-borne cortège. A roofed causeway heading west led to the mortuary temple where funerary rituals and subsequent ceremonies perpetuating the cult of the deceased king were performed. This building abutted the pyramid on its eastern side with a false door. The entrance to the pyramid was in the northern side. The cardinal orientation of the Giza pyramids is extremely accurate: the western and eastern sides of the Great Pyramid of Khufu are aligned almost exactly to true north. Furthermore a straight line runs north-east through the south-east corner of the three pyramids.

The symbolism of the pyramid is primarily solar. The Giza pyramids were mostly originally encased in brilliant white limestone from the nearby Turah quarries. Some of the original limestone, though now dulled by erosion and pollution, is still in place at the apex of Khafra's pyramid. The pyramid of Menkaura was unfinished and not entirely encased; red granite blocks are visible around its base. When the sun, as sun god, hit the limestone-encased pyramids the effect would have been a dazzling statement of the interface between the pharaoh and his heavenly father: such associations with light and rebirth would have demonstrated daily the entombed kings' overcoming of the darkness of the underworld.

The Great Sphinx, fronted by its own unfinished temple and very probably the work of Khafra, faces east. The human-headed lion was a symbol of sovereignty; bathed in dawn sunlight it again demonstrated the king's relationship to the sun god. During the New Kingdom (1550–1069 BC) – over a thousand years later – restoration work on the Sphinx began. A colossal statue of a striding pharaoh may have been placed beneath the beard (part of the latter is now in The British Museum). An extensive mud-brick temple was also built to commemorate the Sphinx under the new title of Horemakhet or Horus-in-the-Horizon.

Features of the classic Old Kingdom pyramid complex included a small satellite pyramid immediately to the south, thought to house the *ka* or spiritual essence of the king, pyramids for queens, boat pits and mastaba tombs for high officials. The mastaba cemeteries next to the Great Pyramid at Giza are rigidly ordered in their layout; the mastabas to the east housed Khufu's relatives and those to the west his high officials.

After the burial of the king a tax-exempt 'pyramid town' developed in the environs. This included houses for priests, farmers and workmen as well as workshops, animal pens and storage magazines. Because the colossal stone-built pyramids have survived relatively well while their associated mud-brick towns have virtually vanished, it is nowadays tempting to view the pyramid as the final burial place of the king and little more. In fact a thriving, virtually autonomous community existed that was dedicated to the perpetuation of the king's cult and hence the validation of the political system which was founded on the notion of divine kingship.

The 4th Dynasty tomb of Queen Khentkawes (c. 2490 BC) was shaped like a gigantic rectangular sarcophagus. Blocks were added to a base of sculpted natural rock. A community that served the deceased queen's cult developed in a town due east of the burial monument.

OPPOSITE *The Great Pyramid was originally just under 147 metres in height and comprised of some 2,300,000 blocks of stone. Though several other pyramids approach Khufu's in terms of size, none matches it in terms of internal complexity and precision of construction. It is unclear whether the three chambers within correspond to changes in plan for the location of the burial chamber, or rather to a unified scheme related to cult practice for the deceased king.*

BELOW *View north to the Great Pyramid from the portico of the mastaba of Rawer, whose titles included Judge, Nome Administrator and Overseer of Works of the King. The (upside down) hieroglyphs are from the false door of the mastaba and are a form of the so-called offering formula whereby the deceased hoped to partake in offerings made by the king to various gods.*

BELOW *Immediately in front of the Great Sphinx is the so-called Dream Stela of Tuthmosis IV (1400–1390 BC). He offers to mirror images of the Sphinx which is named (immediately above its head) Horus-in-the-Horizon. In the text below, the king recounts how he dreamt, before ascending the throne, that if he cleared the sand engulfing the monument he would become king.*

RIGHT *The colossal mortuary temple of the pyramid of Khafra (2558–2532 BC) is now ruined. It incorporated, as did his valley temple and the Sphinx Temple, gigantic limestone blocks. Granite was used extensively to line the inside of the valley temple.*

ABU GHURAB AND ABUSIR

The rulers of the 5th Dynasty (2494–2345 BC) did not attempt to build pyramids on anything like the scale of the greatest builders of the 4th Dynasty. Instead, they emphasized other aspects of the ancient solar religion whose cult centre was at Heliopolis (nowadays buried under the northern suburbs of Cairo). The Westcar Papyrus, probably composed during the Middle Kingdom (some 500 years later) claims that the first three kings of this dynasty – Userkaf, Sahura and Neferirkara – were children of the wife of the Heliopolitan high priest. Whether or not this is true, it demonstrates the need on the part of the later Egyptians to explain not merely the transition from the 4th Dynasty to the 5th, but also the new emphasis on sun worship.

It is known from surviving texts that most of the rulers of the 5th Dynasty built sun temples – innovative structures specifically designed for the worship and celebration of the sun god. Only two of these temples are known today, those of Userkaf and Niuserra at Abu Ghurab, both of which are in very poor condition. Nevertheless their basic features have been reconstructed by archaeologists. Userkaf's sun temple went through several building stages. In its earliest form the central feature may have been a mound (corresponding to the primeval mound of creation established by the sun god) within an enclosure wall. Thereafter this temple was modified by Userkaf's descendants, especially Niuserra who appears to have provided the structure with an obelisk, an impressive valley temple and a connecting causeway. At Niuserra's own sun temple 600 metres to the north-west, the tumbled blocks of the more modest valley temple are visible. The central feature of the temple proper – a massive masonry obelisk some 36 metres tall mounted on a 20-metre-high pedestal – is now little more than a mound of rubble.

Userkaf built his pyramid at Saqqara, but Abusir was chosen by the next five rulers. Sahura's pyramid is the most northern of the conspicuous trio of pyramids at Abusir. The second pyramid to the south is that of his brother and successor Neferirkara. The beginnings of a pyramid structure to the north-west of Sahura's complex has been attributed to Shepseskara, who reigned briefly after Neferirkara. Shepseskara's successor, Raneferef, had his unfinished pyramid completed as a mastaba by Niuserra and it is Niuserra's own pyramid that is positioned between those of Sahura and Neferirkara. Having been stripped of their outer casings in Roman times, the Abusir pyramids are heavily ruined. Extensive high-quality reliefs once decorated Sahura's pyramid complex and magnificently carved hieroglyphs are still to be seen on granite fragments in the mortuary temple.

Several papyrus archives have been found at Abusir. Written in a cursive form of hieroglyphs termed hieratic, they throw considerable light on various aspects of the functioning of the temple cults. In 1893 villagers digging in Neferirkara's complex discovered some 300 fragments. One mentions Raneferef's then unidentified mortuary temple – a mention that led not only to its identification and the discovery of a collection of broken statues therein, but also to the discovery of yet more papyrus documents. Papyri have also been found at the pyramid complex of Queen Khentkawes, the mother of Raneferef and Niuserra. Her complex was built just south of her husband Neferirkara's pyramid and, intriguingly, it functioned as her own cult centre to the end of the next dynasty. It has also yielded papyri. That the cult of Khentkawes should have been perpetuated in regal form (a pyramid complex) raises the question of whether she reigned as queen in her own right or as regent.

View of the sun temple of Niuserra (2445–2421 BC) at Abu Ghurab. In front of the platform that originally held an obelisk is the altar. In the centre is a circle that represents the sun. At the cardinal points is the hieroglyphic sign HETEP *which means offerings; it is the image of a loaf on a mat.*

View through the entrance hall towards the pyramid of Sahura (2487–2475 BC) at Abusir: two (reconstructed) columns with palm capitals stand in the court immediately in front of the remains of the mortuary temple.

Abusir: the pyramid of Neferirkara (2475–2455 BC) is on the left (west) and that of Niuserra (2445–2421 BC) at the end of the causeway. The black basalt causeway of Neferirkara was re-routed to Niuserra's pyramid.

SAQQARA

Saqqara was the necropolis of the nearby ancient capital of Mennefer, known today by its classical name of Memphis. The latter, strategically poised between Upper and Lower Egypt, has virtually vanished: its stone plundered for building material, its mud-brick robbed for fertilizer, slowly but surely coated in alluvium from the Nile, little now remains of this once magnificent city. The history of pharaonic Memphis was intimately connected with the movements of the Nile: as the Nile gradually moved further east in its course, so the ancient city followed.

Saqqara is one of the richest archaeological sites in all of Egypt with impressive remains dating from the 1st Dynasty to the Christian era: the Monastery of Apa Jeremias, south-east of the Step Pyramid, was still occupied in the 9th century AD. Many of the New Kingdom tombs nearby were plundered for the monastery's building material.

The plateau is pockmarked with innumerable, often reused tombs from the Early Dynastic to the Late Period. There are a dozen regal pyramids of the 3rd, 5th, 6th, 8th and 13th Dynasties, and extensive catacombs for bovine, falcon, ibis, jackal, baboon and cat burials. Apis bulls were mummified and buried in gigantic sarcophagi in the Serapeum whose galleries have been dated from the New Kingdom to Ptolemaic times. The discovery of votive tablets associated with these bull burials has contributed to establishing both the reign length and sequence of various rulers.

The most famous monument at Saqqara is the 3rd Dynasty Step Pyramid of King Djoser (2667–2648 BC) that reaches a height of over 60 metres. Designed by the legendary and subsequently deified architect Imhotep, the Step Pyramid is generally considered to be the first large masonry structure in the world – a supposition that has been recently challenged. Immediately to the west of the Step Pyramid enclosure is an even larger, and as yet virtually unexcavated, rectangular area which was originally surrounded by stone walls 15 metres thick. Tentatively attributed via fragments of pottery to the mighty King Khasekhemwy (c. 2686 BC) of the 2nd Dynasty, the massive enclosure walls of this unfinished structure suggest that Djoser was not the first king to build on a large scale in stone even if he was the first to complete his funerary complex entirely in stone.

The Step Pyramid started off as a sizeable mastaba tomb which, over several building stages, was enlarged into the final six-tiered monument. By building in stone (as opposed to mud-brick), Imhotep was creating what was perhaps intended to be a funerary monument that surpassed in both longevity and height whatever the Great Enclosure originally contained. The steps of the pyramid may have also represented a stairway for the king to ascend to heaven. The corbelled burial chambers in the subsequent, 'true' pyramids of Sneferu and in the grand gallery of the Great Pyramid, may evoke the same, now internalized, symbolism.

The late 5th Dynasty pyramid complex of Unas (2375–2345 BC) is located just south of the Step Pyramid enclosure. At a little over 40 metres in height it is the smallest regal Old Kingdom pyramid known. Its significance derives from its internal decoration. This is the first pyramid to include within its passages and chambers examples of the Pyramid Texts: a series of hymns, magical spells, litanies, glorifications and rituals, incised in vertical columns of hieroglyphs. Some of these obscure and often baffling compositions are thought to have originated at the very dawn of Egyptian history and are the earliest religious compositions known.

Little remains of the valley temple of Unas (2375–2345 BC) other than these reconstructed palmiform columns. Behind them the top of the Step Pyramid can be discerned.

BELOW *View of the Step Pyramid complex of Djoser (2667–2648 BC). In the foreground is the* SED*-festival court. This is a simulacrum in stone of the complex wherein the king performed rituals that reinvigorated his rule. A double throne platform (for the thrones of Upper and Lower Egypt) is visible in the foreground and stone versions of tent shrines to gods are behind.*

OPPOSITE *The mastaba tomb of Mereruka, son-in-law and vizier of the pharaoh Teti (2345–2323 BC), is one of the largest at Saqqara. In the sacrificial chamber is this fine portrayal of the deceased nobleman striding forth to partake of offerings.*

BELOW *When he was a general under Tutankhamun (1336–1327 BC) and Ay (1327–1323 BC), Horemheb built a splendid tomb for himself in the New Kingdom necropolis at Saqqara. In this cast of a tomb stela therein (the original was acquired by The British Museum in 1839), Horemheb adores Horakhty, Thoth and Maat. The text below is a great hymn to the traditional gods.*

RIGHT *The builders of the Coptic monastery of Apa Jeremias, an early Christian saint, plundered many New Kingdom blocks for their own buildings. The church, a basilica, was a late feature of the site, and had columns of limestone, marble and granite. The monastery was abandoned in the 9th century AD.*

SOUTHERN PYRAMID FIELDS

The classic pyramid design was perfected by Khufu on the Giza plateau. At 146 metres in height, Khufu's is the largest pyramid ever built. The accuracy of its alignments and the complexity of its internal passages, shafts and chambers certainly make this the greatest of pyramids. However, although Khufu was the builder of the greatest pyramid, he was not the greatest pyramid builder. This honour belongs to his father Sneferu (2613–2589 BC), the first king of the 4th Dynasty.

The two gigantic pyramids at Dahshur – the Bent Pyramid and the Red Pyramid – have been firmly attributed to Sneferu. At a little over 100 metres each in height, their combined volume of over 3 million cubic metres comfortably surpasses that of the Great Pyramid. However, the story does not start at Dahshur. Between the Nile Valley and the Fayum, at Meidum, is the towering wreck of what is, at least in its initial building stages, an even earlier massive pyramid that reached over 90 metres in height. The Meidum Pyramid started as a step pyramid but was completed in the classic, smooth-sided form. Other features at Meidum that were to be seen in later pyramids include a satellite pyramid on the southern side, a corbelled burial chamber, an entrance in the north side of the pyramid and a causeway running east. There is also rudimentary organization within the associated mastaba cemeteries whose plan was subsequently more rigorously adopted by Khufu at Giza.

It used to be thought that disaster befell the Meidum Pyramid: the first impression one has on seeing the core drowning in the pyramid's own rubble is that the outer casing simply collapsed. This supposition has been extended to the Bent Pyramid at Dahshur: if the Meidum Pyramid collapsed during the construction of the Bent Pyramid (whose original angle of elevation of 54 degrees is close to that of Meidum's 52 degrees), then this might explain the sudden change of angle in the upper third of the later pyramid to a less severe 43 degrees. In fact the Bent Pyramid's bend is probably due to the fact that it was sited on unstable clay and cracks were appearing in the structure even before it was finished.

The Meidum Pyramid was previously attributed by default to Huni, the last king of the 3rd Dynasty and Sneferu's father-in-law. It seemed inconceivable that Sneferu could have built three massive pyramids (not to mention a smaller pyramid 9 kilometres west of Meidum at Seila that was probably a cenotaph). However, textual evidence from Meidum – including the ancient name of the pyramid 'Sneferu Endures' – points to Sneferu as its builder. It may be that the conversion of the Meidum Pyramid from a step pyramid to a true pyramid was the culmination of Sneferu's building programme, the true pyramid form being first suggested by the Bent and then realized in the subsequent Red Pyramid of Dahshur. If this is the case, then the combined volume of Sneferu's pyramids is over 3½ million cubic metres.

Archaeologists have not found evidence of the Meidum Pyramid collapsing during the Old Kingdom; indeed, the presence of a contemporary cemetery implies that the collapse, if it occurred, was considerably later, perhaps due to the unfinished pyramid being fatally weakened by quarrying activity. Intriguingly, the Great Pyramid of Khufu has virtually the same angle of slope as the Meidum Pyramid in its final stage. This suggests that when Khufu built his Giza pyramid he looked to the Meidum Pyramid in its terminal form as his model. Which of his three pyramids Sneferu chose to be buried in has not been established.

The Bent Pyramid (centre) and the Red Pyramid (right) at Dahshur were part of Sneferu's (2613–2589 BC) unsurpassed pyramid-building programme. To the left (south) of the Bent Pyramid is its satellite pyramid.

The pyramid complexes of the Middle Kingdom are much ruined. Unlike their Old Kingdom forebears they were not solidly constructed of well-fitted inner blocks. Once their outer casings had been robbed, they rapidly disintegrated. The pyramid of Senwosret I (1965–1920 BC) at el-Lisht had nine subsidiary pyramids and a satellite pyramid. Its burial chamber is flooded and has not been entered by archaeologists.

The pyramid at Meidum was the first started and probably the last completed by Sneferu (2613–2589 BC). At the end of the causeway a small chapel is just visible with two uninscribed stelae.

THE FAYUM

The Fayum is an immensely fertile depression connected to the Nile by the artificially regulated Bahr Yussef canal. In the north-west of the depression is Lake Moeris which has been shrinking in size since Ptolemaic times, leaving many of the ancient sites now isolated from their original lakeside positions. To the north of Lake Moeris, the desert is buttressed by the dramatic scarps of limestone hills. This is in stark contrast to the lush, well-watered, level landscape elsewhere.

The marshes of the ancient Fayum, rich in fish and game, attracted prehistoric hunters. The Greek historian Diodorus Siculus, who visited Egypt from 60–57 BC, recounts the legend that the presumed founder of ancient Egypt, Menes (nowadays tentatively conflated with Narmer), was saved by a crocodile while hunting in the marshes. He therefore declared the crocodiles of the lake protected. However unlikely the story, the crocodile god, in various forms, became the prime focus of worship in Fayum temples through to Roman times, with Shedet (Crocodilopolis) acting as the cult centre.

Something of a backwater during the earlier stages of Pharaonic history, the Fayum first received significant royal attention during the Middle Kingdom when the founder of the 12th Dynasty, Amenemhat I (1985–1955 BC), moved the capital to Amenemhatitjtawy. The city, now buried under cultivation, has not been located, but it was presumably close to the king's pyramid complex at el-Lisht. The Fayum then became something of a royal hunting ground. More significant, however, was Amenemhat I's enlarging of the channel into the lake and his construction of an extensive embankment to block the escape of excess water to the north-east. Thereafter the lake's level began to rise and reached some 18 metres above sea level. During the Ptolemaic Period waterflow into the Fayum was reduced for irrigation purposes and over 1000 square kilometres of rich agricultural land was reclaimed. Due to this, the Middle Kingdom buildings of Medinet Madi and Qasr el-Sagha, and also the 12th Dynasty pyramids in the vicinity are now high and dry. The maintenance of the Ptolemaic irrigation system was rigorously enforced by the state on the rural population. The Fayum basin soon became a prime settlement area and new towns started to appear. Ptolemy II Philadelphus (285–246 BC), for example, settled Graeco-Macedonian veterans here. During the latter centuries of the Roman Period, canal maintenance deteriorated and the desert again encroached; the waters of the lake slowly increased in salinity and the region entered another period of decline.

While ancient Egyptian temples were usually built in stone, most domestic buildings tended to be built in mud-brick. The aridity of the Fayum region and the protective blanket of sand that soon covered the abandoned sites has meant that the mud-brick towns are extremely well preserved. New houses were often built on top of previous uncleared structures resulting in sizeable mounds (*koms*). Archaeologists have been able to reconstruct the evolution of domestic architecture during the Graeco-Roman Period in towns such as Kom Aushim (Karanis) and Dimai (Soknopaiou Nesos).

The influx of Greeks into Egypt following the Macedonian invasion may have resulted in increased literacy in the country: vast amounts of papyri written in both Greek and Egyptian demotic (the final stage of the indigenous cursive script) have been discovered in the ruins of the Fayum towns and villages (and elsewhere) and these throw considerable light on numerous aspects of the society.

At Tell Umm el-Breigat (classical name: Tebtunis) a pair of imposing lions, in Greek style, guard the sacred way leading to the now ruined Ptolemaic temple to the crocodile god Sobek.

ABOVE *At Medinet Madi (classical name: Narmouthis) is another rare Middle Kingdom temple. It has inscriptions identifying its builders as Amenemhat III (1855–1808 BC) and Amenemhat IV (1808–1799 BC). Dedicated to Sobek, Renenutet (a cobra goddess) and Horus, it has Graeco-Roman additions including an avenue of sphinxes.*

ABOVE *Kom Aushim (classical name: Karanis) is a well-preserved mud-brick Graeco-Roman town with two stone temples. This, the so-called Northern Temple, is of Roman date and was dedicated to Sobek, Serapis and Zeus Amun.*

OPPOSITE *The Southern Temple at Kom Aushim is of Ptolemaic and Roman date. A Greek inscription above its entrance is a dedication to Nero (AD 54–68). The temple served the cult of two local crocodile gods, Petesuchos and Pnepheros.*

BELOW *The necropolis at Tuna el-Gebel includes several stone-built tomb chapels of Graeco-Roman date. This one, of Ptolemais, is immediately behind (south of) the larger chapel of Petosiris.*

OPPOSITE *Little of the pharaonic material at el-Ashmunein (classical name: Hermopolis Magna) has survived. The most imposing remains are those of the late Roman Christian basilica, many of whose columns have been re-erected.*

ABYDOS

Abydos is one of the most important archaeological sites in Egypt. The 19th Dynasty (1295–1186 BC) temples of Seti I and his son Ramesses II are nowadays the tourist attractions, but the area was of seminal importance from the dawn of Egyptian history.

By the late Old Kingdom, Abydos had become the major cult centre of the underworld god Osiris. His epithet Khentyimentu, which means 'foremost of westerners' (i.e. ruler of the dead), derives from his amalgamation with the local god of this name. Just under 2 kilometres south-west of Seti I's temple, in the desert, is the Early Dynastic royal cemetery of Umm el-Qaab. The tomb of the 1st Dynasty ruler Djer (c. 3000 BC) was subsequently thought to have been the tomb of Osiris, and Abydos became a place of pilgrimage from the Middle Kingdom on. The vast quantities of votive pottery erroneously left at Djer's tomb by pilgrims gives the site its modern Arabic name of Umm el-Qaab which means 'Mother of Pots'.

A mud-brick temple once stood at Kom el-Sultan, north of Umm el-Qaab. Here the annual Osiris procession began and innumerable funerary monuments as well as stelae were erected by the pious on the plateau to its west.

A cemetery previously presumed to be exclusively Predynastic, Cemetery U, lies to the north of Umm el-Qaab. Recent excavations of the largest tomb have uncovered an impressive structure which also appears to have functioned as a symbolic palace. Within it an ivory sceptre – the specific symbol for a ruler – has been discovered. In one storage room were wine jars imported from the Levant. The earliest known labels bearing the hieroglyphic script have also been discovered here and some of the names on the labels suggest locations in the Delta. These combined points imply some level of control of the north by the south considerably earlier than previously supposed, as well as formalized international trade. The discovery of the hieroglyphic labels also puts back the origin of this script to about 3250 BC, making the Egyptian hieroglyphic script the world's earliest known (an honour previously accorded to the Sumerian).

The temples of Seti I and Ramesses II are probably cenotaph structures whereby the deceased king could be associated with Osiris at Abydos. They are the high point of a tradition of monument building that goes back through the New Kingdom (a temple of Tuthmosis III has recently been discovered) to at least as early as the reign of the Middle Kingdom's Senwosret III (1874–1855 BC). Seti I's exquisite reliefs are amongst the finest surviving; those of Ramesses II (in his own temple and also in his father's where he finished the decoration) are inferior. The details of Seti I's reliefs have allowed scholars to reconstruct the rituals associated with the cult of Osiris while the list of kings in both temples (that from Ramesses II's temple is now in The British Museum) have provided both chronological and political information (for example, Queen Hatshepsut is omitted, as are the 'Amarna' rulers between Amenophis III and Horemheb).

The Osireion, immediately behind Seti I's temple, was built with massive granite blocks that recall the megalithic style of the Old Kingdom. It has been attributed to Seti I because his temple abuts it and appears to repeat the New Kingdom royal tomb/mortuary temple relationship. Certainly Seti I's grandson Merenptah (1213–1203 BC) decorated the descending passage of this enigmatic structure though the Osireion may indeed be considerably more ancient.

The reliefs in the temple of Ramesses II (1279–1213 BC) at Abydos still retain much of their original colour. These androgynous offering bearers have blue skin that symbolizes their fecundity. The central column of hieroglyphs states that Ramesses II has come bringing everything.

BELOW *In the Osiris chapel of his temple at Abydos, Seti I (1294–1279 BC) presents the flail, crook and* WAS*-sceptre, symbols of kingship, to Osiris who grasps the same symbols. The reliefs in this temple are, despite widespread defacement, amongst the finest surviving from ancient Egypt.*

OPPOSITE *Immediately behind Seti I's temple at Abydos, and probably built by him, is the Osireion. Composed of megalithic granite blocks, it perhaps represents the ancient tomb of Osiris. Its depth meant that it would be partly filled with ground water that presumably symbolized the waters from which rebirth and renewal annually occurred.*

DENDERA

Texts demonstrate that there was a temple at Dendera as early as the Old Kingdom (2686–2181 BC). However, the surviving complex of sacred buildings clustered around the massive and well-preserved Temple of Hathor are mostly Graeco-Roman (332 BC–AD 395).

Egyptian temples usually faced the Nile which meant that their orientation was basically east–west. Dendera, however, is located on a bend of the river where it flows east–west; the temple is on the south bank and so unusually points north towards the river.

The *Description de l'Égypte* shows that at the very end of the 18th century the area within the massive, undulating enclosure walls was choked by the mud-brick remains of later buildings. These included structures of the Copts who in the 5th century AD built a fine church between the Roman and 30th Dynasty/Ptolemaic birth houses (small temples celebrating the birth of the child-god). The same Copts also obliterated the faces of the main temple's exquisite Hathor columns and defaced much else besides in an attempt to rid the buildings of their un-Christian imagery. Indeed, in the Christian era Dendera may have been converted into a monastery.

Hathor, often shown in the form of a cow, was one of the greatest of female deities and had numerous cult centres, of which Dendera was the most important. She was goddess of music and the great Hathor columns symbolize her sacred musical instrument, the sistrum.

Hathor was the consort of a form of Horus worshipped at the latter's Graeco-Roman temple at Edfu 190 kilometres upstream. The two temples were ceremonially connected and have complementary reliefs. In the annual Festival of Reunion, the sacred image of Hathor was taken in a flotilla from Dendera to Edfu.

The offspring of the union was Ihy and there were once also temples to both Horus of Edfu and Ihy at Dendera.

A remarkable zodiacal ceiling in a shrine of Osiris on the roof of the Hathor temple was removed in 1821 and is now in the Louvre, Paris. However, still present on the roof is a charming chapel with sistrum capitals. Stored in a series of crypts in the massive southern walls of the temple was the sacred temple equipment, which included a *ba*-figure of Hathor (the *ba* was the soul-like aspect of an individual). During the New Year Festival the figure was taken via a western staircase with ascending reliefs to the aforementioned chapel where, at dawn, it was united with the sun. Then it was returned, via the eastern staircase with descending reliefs, back to its crypt. Hathor's solar aspect is further illustrated on the south wall of the temple where a massive, presumably once gilded, relief of her sistrum rests above the hieroglyphic sign for gold. This too fell victim to Coptic defacement. The central location of this image aligns with the *naos* or shrine of the goddess inside the temple: this was the culmination of the symbolic route of the sun god within the temple. The exterior of the south-facing wall also has massive portrayals of the legendary queen Cleopatra VII Philopator and her son by Julius Caesar and future co-regent, Ptolemy XV Caesarion (44–30 BC).

The king was associated with the falcon god Horus. Indeed, the name Hathor actually means 'House of Horus' and is written in hieroglyphs with a falcon (Horus) within the sign for a mansion or enclosure. Furthermore, the word for palace, *setep-sa*, suggests that the concept of palace derived from the place where the choicest (*setep*) of cows resided (*sa* is a byre). The cow goddess Hathor was, at one level, the mother of the king: part of the king's regalia included the wearing of a bull's tail.

A gate of Domitian (AD 81–96) and Trajan (AD 98–117) stands at the entrance to the Hathor Temple at Dendera (classical name: Tentyris). The undulating walls that enclose the temple probably symbolize the waves of the primeval waters from which order (represented by the temple) arose.

ABOVE *A Christian basilica was built at Dendera in the Roman Period between the two birth houses. Its plan is similar to the churches of two major monasteries near Sohag, suggesting that Dendera was once an important monastery site.*

OPPOSITE *The quality, complexity and state of preservation of the reliefs of the Roman birth house at Dendera, built by Augustus (30 BC–AD 14) and decorated by Tiberius (AD 14–37), are all remarkable. Here Ihy, the offspring of the union between Hathor and Horus, is celebrated. In the central scene he is portrayed both as a suckling infant and as an adult-sized child behind Hathor.*

LUXOR: *Karnak Temple Complex*

The bewildering scale of the remains within the enclosure wall at Karnak makes it the most impressive of Upper Egyptian sites. It became the cult centre of the god Amun from the time of the Middle Kingdom, when Amun superseded Montu as the principal local diety. With the Theban origin of the New Kingdom monarchs, Amun, long associated with the ancient Heliopolitan sun god Ra in the form of Amun-Ra, was promoted to national supremacy.

The bulk of the remains date to the New Kingdom as successive rulers extended and elaborated the main temple to this amalgamated version of the new state god. The Amun-Ra complex is laid out along two converging axes. The original symbolic west–east axis is essentially solar in orientation: six pylons with associated courts, shrines, obelisks and colossi lead to the small, dark sanctuary which, in its surviving form, dates to Philip Arrhidaeus (323–317 BC), half-brother of Alexander the Great.

After abandoning the traditional religion, Akhenaten (1352–1336 BC), whose followers defaced the name of Amun at Karnak, early in his reign built a (now destroyed) temple to the solar disc, his new sole god, immediately to the east of the Amun-Ra enclosure. The location was presumably chosen on symbolic grounds: his temple was nearer to the dawn sun. The restoration of the orthodox religion under Horemheb (1323–1295 BC) meant the dismantling of this temple (and others built by Akhenaten at Thebes) whose small blocks or *talatat* were used in Horemheb's Karnak structures. By 1965 some 45,000 decorated *talatat* blocks had been discovered in Horemheb's pylons and under the hypostyle hall of the main temple. This latter structure, presumably conceived by Horemheb but

essentially the work of Seti I and his son Ramesses II, represents on stupendous scale, with its forest of plant columns, the primeval swamp at the dawn of the orthodox account of creation. Flanked by 122 columns topped with closed papyrus buds, the central, processional west–east avenue consists of twelve columns each 21 metres in height topped with open papyrus capitals.

To the symbolic west of this is a large open court fronted by an unfinished pylon probably dating to the 30th Dynasty (380–343 BC). Within the court is a single standing column from a kiosk of the 25th Dynasty (Nubian) pharaoh Taharko (690–664 BC), a triple barque shrine of Seti II (1200–1194 BC) and, extending through the southern wall, an impressive temple and barque shrine of Ramesses III (1184–1153 BC).

The north–south axis of the Amun-Ra complex consists of a series of pylons culminating in a pylon of Horemheb (according to modern numbering, Pylon 10) embedded in the enclosure wall. To the south, and connected by an avenue of ram-headed sphinxes, is a temple complex to Mut, the vulture goddess and consort of Amun.

Other structures within the 123 hectares of the enclosed area include, in the western corner, a Graeco-Roman temple of the hippopotamus goddess Opet and a late New Kingdom temple of Khonsu (son of Amun and Mut); a rectangular sacred lake to the south-west of the sanctuary of the Amun-Ra complex; and a New Kingdom temple of Ptah just inside the north-eastern enclosure wall. East of the shrine of Philip Arrhidaeus is a Middle Kingdom courtyard and beyond this is Tuthmosis III's (1479–1425 BC) festival hall or *Akhmenu*.

North-east of the Amun-Ra complex is a New Kingdom temple dedicated to the war god Montu. Avenues of rams and of human-headed sphinxes lead from the Amun-Ra enclosure south-west to Luxor Temple.

The temple complex of Karnak at Luxor (classical name: Thebes) was enlarged by successive New Kingdom monarchs. The second pylon was, in the 19th Dynasty (1295–1186 BC), the entrance to the main temple along its solar axis. The statues are of Ramesses II (1279–1213 BC).

OPPOSITE *At the north of the Karnak complex is this charming 18th Dynasty (1550–1295 BC) temple of Ptah which is approached by a series of five Ptolemaic gates. Its northern location in the compound may be in deference to Ptah's cult centre at Memphis (to the north). Kings on the north side of the gates wear the red crown of Lower (northern) Egypt, those on the south, the white crown of Upper (southern) Egypt.*

BELOW *These heads of Amun (left) and Amunet have the stylistic features of Tutankhamun (1336–1327 BC). Amun and his consort were two of the original Ogdoad (group of eight) creator gods of Hermopolis Magna. The pair personify invisibility and were associated with Amun of Thebes, hence their appearance at Karnak. The obelisk of Hatshepsut (1473–1458 BC) is behind.*

BELOW *In the foreground is the exquisite Middle Kingdom kiosk of Senwosret I (1965–1920 BC) which was found dismantled in the third pylon of Karnak, built by Amenophis III (1390–1352 BC). Behind it are similarly reconstructed early New Kingdom examples.*

OPPOSITE *At the eastern end of the solar axis of the Amun Temple, Ramesses II (1279–1213 BC) erected an east-facing temple to Amun-Ra-Horakhty. This may have served for the petitions of the populace who were barred from the main temple precinct.*

LUXOR: *Luxor Temple*

Luxor Temple became, during the New Kingdom (1550–1069 BC), central to the pharaoh's identification with the primordial creator. The temple was primarily concerned with the fertility aspects of Amun in the form of Amun-Min. The pharaoh was son and earthly counterpart of the creator god: one of the chambers of the inner temple has a relief scene in which Queen Mutemwia, the wife of Tuthmosis IV (1400–1390 BC), is shown in sexual union with Amun-Ra, the result being the next pharaoh Amenophis III (1390–1352 BC).

The pharaoh was responsible for the fertility and well-being of Egypt. At Luxor Temple the Opet Festival evolved to demonstrate and validate this. It was held during the inundation (the annual flooding of the Nile) because this was the time of fertility and renewal. The cult image of Amun was transported from Karnak 2½ kilometres to the north-east to Luxor Temple. In the dimly lit inner sanctum of Luxor Temple rituals were performed whereby the king's connections with the primordial god were substantiated. Sired by the god, the king had likewise become king via a supernatural process: during the coronation ceremony the sun god invigorated the king with the specifically regal variety of the life-force termed the *ka*. The monarch, as son, counterpart and sole direct recipient of the sun god's divine life-force, embodied and projected justice, order, stability and fertility into the world. The symbolism of the process of embodiment, still visible in the reliefs of the inner barque shrine of Luxor Temple, associated primordial creation with male sexual potency.

Monarchs whose claims to the throne were less than traditional are known to have been particularly active at Luxor Temple. The female pharaoh Hatshepsut (1473–1458 BC) is thought to have elaborated the original ceremonies which demonstrated that the incumbent was the rightful ruler. Ramesses II (1279–1213 BC) incorporated her shrine into the north-eastern corner of his peristyle court perhaps in deference to her religious innovations (pharaohs were notoriously fond of demolishing the structures of their forebears).

Horemheb (1323–1295 BC), the non-royal general who re-established the traditional religion after the upheaval of the Amarna Period, chose, unusually, Luxor Temple (rather than Memphis) for his coronation. This occurred at dawn: when the newly crowned king emerged from between the temple pylons into the profane world, he symbolized, as son of the sun god, the *akhet* or sun rising at dawn between two mountains. He was the earthly embodiment of the solar falcon Ra-Horakhty and his reign, from the dawn of the coronation to the dusk of death, would parallel the flight of the solar falcon. Alexander the Great, who invaded Egypt in 332 BC, chose to restore the inner barque shrine of Luxor Temple – the very font of New Kingdom kingship – while, intriguingly, leaving the Karnak complex untouched. He was unambiguously associating his presence with the greatest pharaohs.

The main axis of Luxor Temple is orientated at a right-angle to the main axis of the Amun Temple at Karnak. This relationship is thought to have provided the prototype of subsequent Graeco-Roman temples such as those at Edfu and Dendera whose own birth houses are similarly orientated, though the format became compressed into a far more modest scale.

The major pharaonic builders at Luxor Temple were Amenophis III (the inner temple, sun court and massive columns of the colonnade), Tutankhamun (1336–1327 BC) (who may have built but certainly decorated most of the colonnade's enclosing walls) and Ramesses II (the peristyle court and pylon).

The pylon of Luxor Temple dates to Ramesses II (1279–1213 BC). Its outer face records the Battle of Kadesh against the Hittites in the fifth year of his reign. During the Roman Period (30 BC–AD 395) the temple was converted into a military camp: the small chapel of Serapis on the right is of this time.

LUXOR: *West Bank Mortuary Temples*

Numerous New Kingdom monarchs built what we now call mortuary temples along a stretch of the West Bank, directly opposite the area demarcated by the temples of Karnak and Luxor on the opposite bank of the Nile. The pharaohs termed these their 'Temples of Millions of Years'; they were created to perpetuate the deceased king's cult which would in turn provide nourishment for the dead king's *ka*. During the annual Festival of the Valley, statues of Amun, Mut and Khonsu – the Theban Triad – left the Karnak enclosure and visited the temples of Deir el-Bahari (exactly opposite Karnak) before progressing to the mortuary temple of the incumbent king. Nowadays the most southern, that of Ramesses III (1184–1153 BC) at Medinet Habu, and the most northern, that of Seti I (1294–1279 BC) near the hill of Dra Abu el-Naga, are still partly standing. The two other relatively well-preserved New Kingdom royal mortuary temples are those of Hatshepsut (1473–1458 BC) at Deir el-Bahari and that of Ramesses II (1279–1213 BC) (the Ramesseum) just over a kilometre north-east of Medinet Habu. It may be that the Ramesseum's curious parallelogram structure is designed to orientate it towards Luxor Temple.

The basic features of the New Kingdom mortuary temple may have originated with Hatshepsut. These include a chapel to Osiris/the deceased/his ancestors in the symbolic western side, a cult chapel dedicated to the sun god on the symbolic eastern side, and a sanctuary to Amun at the back of the temple on its central axis.

The enormous mud-brick storerooms surrounding the Ramesseum reveal the significance of the mortuary temples as powerful, autonomous economic units after the death of the king. The best preserved, that of Ramesses III at Medinet Habu, owes its survival to a variety of factors. After the death of Ramesses III, the site functioned as the administrative capital of the West Bank, while its enormous defensive walls provided security during periods of political unrest.

Outstanding commoners were allowed, very occasionally, to build mortuary temples. Examples are Amenophis, son of Hapu, the architect of Amenophis III (1390–1352 BC) and Nebwenenef, the first prophet of Amun under Ramesses II.

Evolved from the mortuary temples of Old and Middle Kingdom pyramid complexes, the New Kingdom royal mortuary temples were not the first such structures to be built on the West Bank: the relatively well-preserved mortuary temple of the founder of the Middle Kingdom, Mentuhotep II (2055–2004 BC), is to be found south of Hatshepsut's mortuary temple at Deir el-Bahari (a temple of Tuthmosis III once stood between the two). Mentuhotep II's temple, predating Hatshepsut's by half a millennium, is its architectural ancestor. This innovative temple was laid out in a series of terraces. Its colonnaded, open plan recalls the so-called *saff* tombs at el-Tarif (north of Seti I's mortuary temple) built by Mentuhotep II's immediate 11th Dynasty forebears. The cult chapel of the king, located against the cliff, and the hypostyle hall that fronted it, are now destroyed. Unlike the subsequent New Kingdom mortuary temples, Mentuhotep II's also functioned as a tomb for the monarch and his family whereas the New Kingdom monarchs were buried apart from their mortuary temples in the Valley of the Kings. The logic of their burial place is, however, apparent: the Valley of the Kings is immediately behind the cliffs of Deir el-Bahari and Hatshepsut's own tomb (KV 20) is located on the same axis as her mortuary temple in the opposite face of the same rock formation.

The Colossi of Memnon – so-called by the Greeks – once stood in front of the entrance of the now vanished mortuary temple of Amenophis III (1390–1352 BC). Damaged by an earthquake in 27 BC, the northern statue (in the foregound) used to moan in the dawn breeze.

ABOVE *View out to the cultivation from the entrance pylon of the Ramesseum (the mortuary temple of Ramesses II (1279–1213 BC)). This was the first mortuary temple whose pylon was built in stone. Its foundations were continually weakened by flood water and it has partially collapsed.*

OPPOSITE *This colossal head belonged to one of a pair of statues that stood in the colonnaded second court of the Ramesseum before the entrance to the hypostyle hall. Osiriform statues of the king line the east and west sides of the court, perhaps in reference to the sun's journey.*

The name Ozymandias, immortalized in Shelley's sonnet, probably derives from Ramesses II's prenomen User-Maat-Ra. At the edge of the second court of the Ramesseum is the fallen red granite statue of the poem. Originally 20 metres tall and weighing more than 1000 tonnes, this may be the largest statue ever sculpted in Egypt.

View north towards the large hypostyle hall of the Ramesseum. In the lower relief of the shattered block in the foreground, Ramesses II wears the ATEF *crown. This consists of ram horns, ostrich plumes and a central bushel of wheat topped with the sun disc. This crown was associated with Osiris, fertility and renewal.*

OPPOSITE *View out through the large hypostyle hall of the Ramesseum towards the fallen 'Ozymandias' colossus and pylon. Like the great hypostyle hall at Karnak, the central avenue of the Ramesseum's has large columns topped with open papyriform capitals. Smaller columns with closed papyrus buds flank them.*

ABOVE *The mortuary temple of Ramesses III (1184–1153 BC) at Medinet Habu is closely modelled on the Ramesseum and far better preserved. Before the first pylon (to the left) is a relief of Shepenwepet II on the outer wall of her tomb chapel. She was one of the Divine Adoratrices, a series of priestesses of the 25th and 26th Dynasties (747–525 BC) who held considerable political power in the Theban region.*

ABOVE The figures in the antechamber of the tomb of Horemheb are generally better proportioned than those in the well shaft and the dark background of the former has been replaced by a more pale grey. This perhaps represents the first light of dawn/rebirth. Here the Osiris Horemheb is before the underworld god Anubis.

OPPOSITE *The burial chamber of Ramesses I's tomb has texts and scenes from the underworld book known as the Book of Gates. The upper scene shows a ram-headed sun god in the solar barque accompanied by the god Sia (Perception) in the prow and Heka (Magic) in the stern. In the lower scene the god Atum-Ra fights Apophis the underworld demon.*

BELOW *The western wall of the burial chamber of Ramesses I's tomb is dominated by the seated figures of Osiris on the right (an officiating* IUNMUTEF *priest stands in front of him), and a scarab-headed version of the sun god on the left.*

OPPOSITE *The decorations in the tomb of Ramesses VI (1143–1136 BC) are often bewilderingly compressed and complex. This scene is from the Eleventh Division of the Book of Gates. In the middle scene, the solar barque is towed by four beings. Five human-headed and four jackal-headed gods, carrying knives and crooks, confront the malevolent serpent Apophis who is chained to the ground.*

ABOVE *In the burial chamber of Ramesses VI's tomb are scenes from the Book of the Earth. Here, in the lower register, the earth god Aker is portrayed as the two sphinxes of dusk and dawn. On the right the solar barque enters the underworld and is grasped by the earth god Tatenen. In the centre, in a realm of mummies, the arms of Nun, goddess of the primeval waters, hold up the sun disc. On the left, the solar barque is dragged out of the underworld by goddesses with the bodies of cobras.*

OPPOSITE *Late in the reign of Amenophis III (1390–1352 BC), the art of raised relief work reached its apex and murals were unpainted to emphasize the quality of the relief work. The tomb of Ramose, Amenophis III's vizier, illustrates this with these figures at a funerary feast. The tomb is of considerable historical importance because Ramose also served Akhenaten (1352–1336 BC) early in the latter's reign, and Amarna-style portrayals coexist with traditional depictions in the tomb.*

ABOVE *This scene from Ramose's tomb juxtaposes the rigidly classical with the more fluid Amarnan style. On the left, funerary equipment is being brought into the tomb by the stilted figures of traditional portrayal. On the right, the majority of female mourners are sinuous and convincing in their grief. But embedded within their group are five figures frozen in the artificial, parallel pose of traditional depiction.*

THE OASES OF EL-KHARGA AND EL-DAKHLA

The oases of the Western Desert were inhabited from at least Middle Palaeolithic times (some 50,000 years ago) when the climate was considerably less harsh and the landscape a savannah. Thereafter desiccation set in resulting, presumably, in reduced, isolated populations closely associated with the oases: little, if any contact is likely to have occurred with the Nile Valley population. From about 7000 BC the desert again became more benign and cattle pastoralists roamed the savannah. It has been supposed that the extreme importance of bovine symbolism in the religion and culture of pharaonic Egypt derived from the influx into the Nile Valley of such people.

Siwa Oasis, located 550 kilometres west of Cairo and almost on the Libyan border, has earned immortality because of Alexander the Great's visit in 331 BC. Having founded Alexandria, the Macedonian conqueror and his small retinue followed the coast west to Paraetonium (Mersa Matruh) before entering the desert and heading the 300 kilometres south for Siwa. The desert journey nearly ended in disaster but a serendipitous storm allowed the group to replenish their water supplies, and crows and talking snakes supposedly guided them in the right direction when they became lost. At the 26th Dynasty (664–525 BC) Temple of Ammon (a ram god presumably related to Amun of Thebes), Alexander was confirmed as the son of Amun, whom the Greeks identified with Zeus: thus he was proclaimed both the son of Zeus and the new pharaoh.

The historically more important oases of the Western Desert are considerably closer to the Nile Valley. The largest is el-Kharga, 200 kilometres west of Esna. The other major oases are el-Dakhla, 150 kilometres west of el-Kharga and, to the north, Farafra and el-Bahariya.

The major caravan routes to Nubia passed by these oases and by the Old Kingdom (2686–2181 BC) they were policed under the supervision of the Egyptian governor at el-Dakhla. Official contact with the oases presumably diminished during periods of political unrest; they were also a refuge for outlaws fleeing the Nile Valley. Early in the Middle Kingdom (2055–1650 BC), troops were sent from victorious Thebes to el-Dakhla to round up the fugitive soldiers of the 10th Dynasty Herakleopolitan armies whose defeat resulted in renewed unification of the country.

Although it has suffered recently from rising groundwater and has been encased in scaffolding, the Temple of Amun at Hibis is the best preserved el-Kharga temple. The earliest parts – or at least their decorations – date to Darius I (522–486 BC) of the 27th Dynasty (also known as the First Persian Period). The majority of other sites at el-Kharga date to the Ptolemaic Period and later, and include the rarely visited yet exquisite temples of Dush, el-Ghueita and Zaiyan.

Although there are cemeteries and settlements from as early as the Old Kingdom at el-Dakhla Oasis, there are few impressive monumental remains. During the 1st century AD, Roman policy in el-Dakhla focused on agricultural development. The recently restored temple of Deir el-Hagar originates from the reign of the Roman emperor Nero (AD 54–68) and was the religious aspect of the development policy which was designed to attract settlers.

Though el-Bahariya Oasis has few standing ancient monuments, the avalanche of burial discoveries that started in 1996, including innumerable Graeco-Roman mummies in a cemetery and the (re)discovery of a series of painted pharaonic tombs, means that the history of this oasis is being dramatically rewritten.

On the left is part of the façade of the original temple of Hibis at el-Kharga Oasis built by Darius I (522–486 BC). Darius I is portrayed as an infant being suckled by the goddess Mut. In his right hand he grasps a crook (the symbol of rulership) and a lapwing bird (the symbol of the populace).

The stone sanctuary and many of the associated mud-brick structures of Qasr Zaiyan, a few kilometres south-east of el-Ghueita, survive. An inscription dates to Antoninus Pius (AD 138–161) and there is also a surviving Ptolemaic lintel. The temple was dedicated to Amun of Hibis, to Mut and to Khonsu.

The early importance of el-Dakhla Oasis, not least its strategic position in terms of desert trade routes, is attested by the sizeable mastabas of its Old Kingdom governors at Balat. This is the excavated mastaba of Khentika, governor of the oasis under Pepi II (2278–2184 BC).

ABOVE AND OPPOSITE *The significance of el-Dakhla Oasis grew with the Roman occupation, when the farming potential of the oasis was optimized. Monumental remains are, however, scant. The upper levels of the desert hills at el-Mazawwaqa are pockmarked with tier upon tier of Roman tomb chambers. Some of the tombs are decorated. At Esbet Bashendi, stone-built Roman funerary houses and their sarcophagi are backed by the mud-brick domed tomb of the medieval holy man Bash Endi, from whom the village derives its name.*

THE GRAECO-ROMAN TEMPLES OF ESNA, EDFU AND KOM OMBO

The Greek and Roman rulers of Egypt revived the ancient temple-building tradition in order to demonstrate their place in the traditional scheme of kingship. However, while the basic aspects of the architectural design can be understood in traditional terms, the development of elaborate reliefs filling every available space to illustrate obscure myths, cult ceremonies and astronomical information was a new development. Furthermore, the accompanying text was often composed in novel, cryptographic hieroglyphs of virtually impenetrable obscurity.

The best preserved and most traditional Graeco-Roman temple is the imposing Temple of Horus at Edfu. This grandiose structure replaced earlier temples in what was the traditional cult centre of the god Horus: it was here that he defeated his great enemy Seth. Extensive inscriptions describe the building of the temple: it was founded by Ptolemy III Euergetes I in 237 BC and it took almost 200 years to complete. Within the sacred innermost complex of rooms and chapels is the *naos,* a shrine of black syenite dated to Nectanebo II (360–343 BC) that presumably derived from an earlier temple. This would have held the cult image of the god. The sanctuary that contains the *naos* connects to the higher and wider *pronaos* which is packed with columns (its ancestor was the New Kingdom hypostyle hall). The outermost columns of the *pronaos* façade are connected by screen walls, a Graeco-Roman innovation, as is the discontinuous lintel of the *pronaos* gateway. Outside is an imposing columned courtyard. Another Graeco-Roman innovation at Edfu is the bewildering variety of plants portrayed in the differ-

ent column capitals throughout the temple. In their original colours they would have symbolized the fecundity of the Nile Valley that rose in response to the overhead sun.

Doors lead from the colonnaded court into the ambulatory, an encircling passage between the outer walls of the temple and its surrounding wall. Inscriptions here announce that the design, intended to protect the temple from the outside world, derives from the sacred rules of temple architecture laid down by Imhotep, the deified architect of the 3rd Dynasty Step Pyramid at Saqqara.

At Esna, 50 kilometres downstream from Edfu, the columned hall (*pronaos*) of a temple dedicated primarily to the divine potter Khnum, survives; other parts of the temple are unexcavated and the modern town is some 9 metres above the floor of the temple. The rear (west) wall of the grand *pronaos* was the façade of the Ptolemaic temple while the columned hall itself was built in the reign of the Roman emperor Claudius (AD 41–54) and decorated into the 3rd century AD. It is thus a very late structure. Of particular interest to scholars are the hymns to Khnum and the temple's festival lists recorded on the twenty-four columns.

On an impressive promontory of the river at Kom Ombo, 60 kilometres south of Edfu, are the remains of the dual temple to the triad of the crocodile god Sobek (on the symbolic east side) and the triad of Haroeris or Horus-the-Elder (on the symbolic west side). It follows the basic Graeco-Roman plan now doubled for the worship of two sets of gods. Ptolemy VI Philometor (180–164 and 163–145 BC) is the earliest named king here though work on the complex continued into Roman times.

At Esna (classical name: Latopolis) the temple façade (1st century AD) is comprised of standard features of the larger Graeco-Roman temple design. These include screen walls connecting the outer columns and the discontinuous lintel of the doorway.

The columns of the PRONAOS of Esna end in a variety of elaborate, stylized plant capitals. The ceiling is decorated with astronomical MOTIFS. The decorative themes of Graeco-Roman temples presumably derived from excerpts from their own libraries.

OPPOSITE *At Edfu (classical name: Apollinopolis Magna) scenes on the towers of the temple pylon are virtually mirror images of each other. In the lower register Ptolemy XII Neos Dionysos (80–58 BC and 55–51 BC) smites stylized bundles of enemies before Horus and Hathor. The hands of the deities stretch out symbolically to the recesses that once held flagpoles: the hieroglyphic sign for a god was a flag fluttering on its pole.*

OPPOSITE *In a depiction at Kom Ombo that originates in the pharaonic era, conquered towns are named within ovals depicting their fortifications and personified by bound and tethered captives. Above, a devouring lion has been added to the traditional pharaonic scene of the monarch smiting captives.*

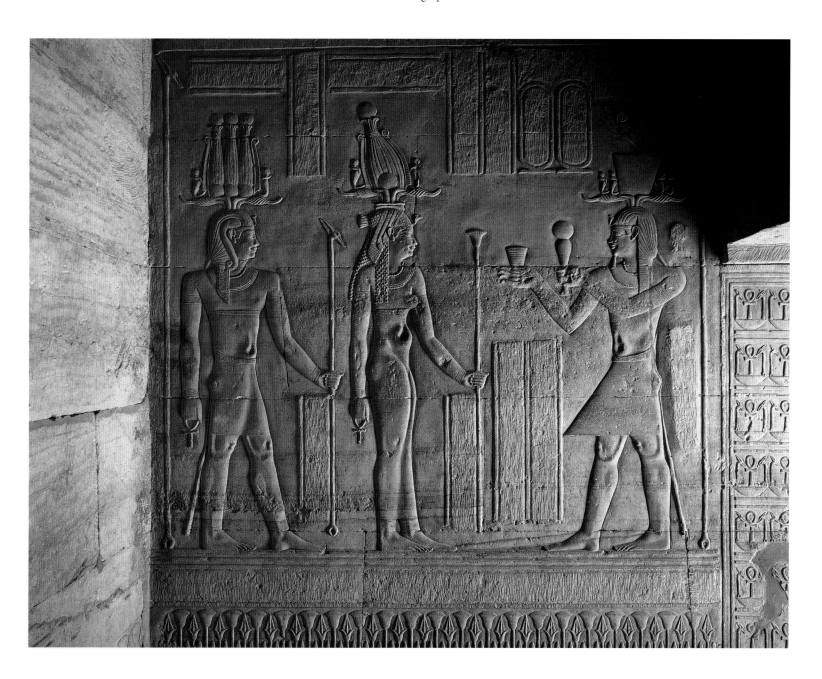

ABOVE *At the rear of the sanctuaries at Kom Ombo are six rooms that were built into the inner face of the inner wall of the ambulatory. In this scene a monarch offers to a goddess and a god. Areas for text have been demarcated but were never completed.*

PHILAE

The impressive granite outcrops of the region of the First Cataract form a natural barrier across the Nile, a barrier whose strategic importance was early recognized. This marked the southern border for much of Egypt's ancient history. The administrative, defensive and trade centre was the island of Elephantine opposite the modern town of Aswan. An entrepôt for the produce of equatorial Africa, the ancient Egyptian name *Abu* (from which Elephantine is derived) means ivory/elephant; the word ivory is possibly descended from it. Thus the name may recall the importance of the ivory trade. Another word for an African trade item that has survived into modern usage is 'ebony'; the Egyptian word was *hebeny*. Though rich in archaeological importance, the ancient remains on the island of Elephantine are fragmentary.

The situation at Philae is spectacularly different: it was the most important cult centre for Isis in the Graeco-Roman world and the evocative remains made this the prime tourist site for travellers in Egypt in the 19th century. With the building of the first Aswan Dam, completed in 1902, the monuments were submerged by the collected flood waters every year from December to August. Thirty years later, when the height of the dam was raised, all but the highest parts became submerged for even longer. With the building of the High Dam (1960–1971) south of Philae, there was not only a danger that the island, trapped between the two dams, would become permanently submerged, but also that its structures would be destroyed by the currents from the new dam. The solution was both radical and successful: the higher, nearby island of Agilkia was reshaped to look like Philae. A coffer dam was built around the latter and the water pumped out.

The buildings were dismantled, moved block by block and reconstructed (in better condition than before despite the loss of their paint) on the nearby island.

During the operation, blocks from earlier structures were found to have been reused in later buildings. New Kingdom blocks were found in structures of Nectanebo I (380–362 BC) of the 30th Dynasty. These earlier blocks were probably imported from elsewhere. Dismantled structures of the 26th (Saite) Dynasty (664–525 BC) were also found in the foundations of later buildings, as was a block of the 25th (Nubian) Dynasty ruler Taharqo (690–664 BC).

The smaller temples on Philae are dedicated to a variety of gods and goddesses – to the Nubian gods Arensnuphis and Mandulis, to Imhotep, Hathor and Harendotus (Horus-the-Avenger). The main temple is dedicated to Isis (a nearby island was dedicated to her husband Osiris). The imposing first pylon is late Ptolemaic (1st century BC) and shows Ptolemy XII Neos Dionysos in traditional pose smiting cowering enemies in front of approving Egyptian gods and goddesses. The defacement of the figures, and the chiselling out of representations of exposed skin, attest to the conversion of the temple into a Christian church. During the Roman Period, the cult of Isis spread throughout the Roman world and was a major rival to Christianity for a time. On the island of Philae, Christian churches were built in the 4th century AD north of the still active Isis Temple. But by the 6th century AD the end had come for the old religion: the columned hall of the Temple of Isis was converted into a church and crosses were chiselled into the stone. An inscription of Bishop Theodorus commends the defacement of the pagan reliefs carried out during the reign of the Byzantine Emperor Justinian (AD 527–565), when the cult of Isis ended.

View across the courtyard towards the first pylon of the Temple of Isis at New Philae. The kiosk from which this photograph was taken was the work of Nectanebo I (380–362 BC).

OPPOSITE *East of the Temple of Isis at New Philae is a charming Ptolemaic temple of Hathor dated to the middle of the 2nd century* BC. *Hathor was associated with joy, celebration and childbirth, and the reliefs include portrayals of Bes the dwarf god who was also associated with childbirth.*

BELOW *The Temple of Isis at Philae became the major cult centre for the goddess throughout the Roman Empire. Her attributes were both ancient and varied and meant that she was identified with the major goddesses of the Graeco-Roman pantheon. The cult of Isis was the major rival to the spread of Christianity whose own Virgin Mary shared many of her attributes.*

OPPOSITE AND BELOW *The Kiosk of Trajan (*AD 98–117*) is the most famous of Philae's monuments and has long inspired artists to sketch and paint it. Its unusual appearance, due to the massive, plain blocks above the floral capitals of its columns, derives from its unfinished state. The original intention would have been to carve these blocks into sistrum capitals echoing those of Nectanebo I's kiosk at the south of the island.*

LOWER NUBIAN SITES

Nubia, the region between the First Cataract (south of Aswan) and the Sixth Cataract (which is north of Khartoum), had a fluctuating relationship with Egypt. Trade between the two regions existed well before Dynastic Egypt came into existence. By the time of the Old Kingdom (2686–2181 BC), Egyptian expeditions were already entering Lower Nubia, or *Wawat*, to trade or mine.

The relationship between Middle Kingdom Egypt (2055–1650 BC) and Nubia was based on a massive Egyptian military presence. During the 12th Dynasty a spectacular sequence of fortresses was built in Lower Nubia as far south as the Semna Gorge, the southern end of the Second Cataract region, so that the pharaoh's imperial monopoly on trade could be enforced.

Following the collapse of the Middle Kingdom, the Egyptian forts were occupied by Kushites (Nubians from the south) who advanced into the power vacuum left by the retreating Egyptians. However, early in the New Kingdom (1550–1069 BC), Egyptian armies advanced as far as the Fourth Cataract (700 kilometres upstream of the Middle Kingdom border) and obliterated any major indigenous threats. The last serious uprisings were quelled by Tuthmosis III (1479–1425 BC), and Nubia downstream of the Fourth Cataract was incorporated into Egypt. Nubians in the occupied territory adopted Egyptian customs and minimally fortified Egyptian temple towns were established.

The Egyptian presence in Nubia did not survive the end of the New Kingdom and Egypt herself was not to know large-scale political unity again until Kushite kings invaded. These kings, the 25th Dynasty (747–656 BC), embraced an Egyptian culture centred on the Amun cult. The Nubian rule lasted a century and was ended by the invasion of the Assyrian king Ashurbanipal who in 663 BC drove the last Kushite pharaoh Tanutamani back into Upper Nubia. Thereafter, an isolated Nubian kingdom centred at Meroe (between the Fifth and Sixth Cataracts) gradually grew in power, its sphere of influence extending ever further northwards: the Meroitic ruler Arqamani and Ptolemy IV Philopator (221–205 BC) collaborated to build temples at Philae and el-Dakka.

During the course of the 20th century Lower Nubia was gradually submerged by the expanding reservoir eventually named Lake Nasser. Sites that could not be removed, such as cemeteries and the Middle Kingdom forts, were surveyed and excavated before being submerged. Five temples were donated to foreign countries. The present remains at New Kalabsha, New Sebua, New Amada and New Abu Simbel are structures rebuilt on higher ground.

The larger temple of Abu Simbel is not only the greatest surviving Nubian monument, but one of the most spectacular in all of Egypt. It was built by Ramesses II (1279–1213 BC) in the first half of his reign and is an enormous example of the rock-cut shrine that was common in Nubia. Its basic form is, however, traditionally Egyptian: four colossi front a pylon-shaped façade excised from the rock face. In the centre, where the sun rises in the symbolism of the *akhet,* is the solar falcon Ra-Horakhty. Within is a larger and then a smaller columned hall that lead to the sanctuary of four gods: Ptah, Amun, the deified Ramesses II and Ra-Horakhty. The magazines that surrounded a normal temple are here recreated as underground storage chambers leading off the central axis. Even in innovation a coherent relationship with the past was preserved.

The Kiosk of Qertassi, now located at New Kalabsha, originally stood 30 kilometres south of the High Dam, at the entrance to ancient quarries. The sistrum capitals declare that it was dedicated to Hathor, patroness of miners. Of Roman date, it is uninscribed and unfinished.

The austere symmetry of Kalabsha Temple is in stark contrast to the arid wilderness of its new location. It is the largest standing temple after the Great Temple of Abu Simbel. The construction, which probably replaced a New Kingdom temple, is of late Ptolemaic date, while the incomplete decoration is early Roman.

Kalabsha Temple is of traditional form: a peristyle court fronts the PRONAOS. *The temple was dedicated to the Lower Nubian god Mandulis who was associated with Horus. Before being flooded by the original Aswan Dam, the garish colours of the reliefs in the rear of the temple were still visible.*

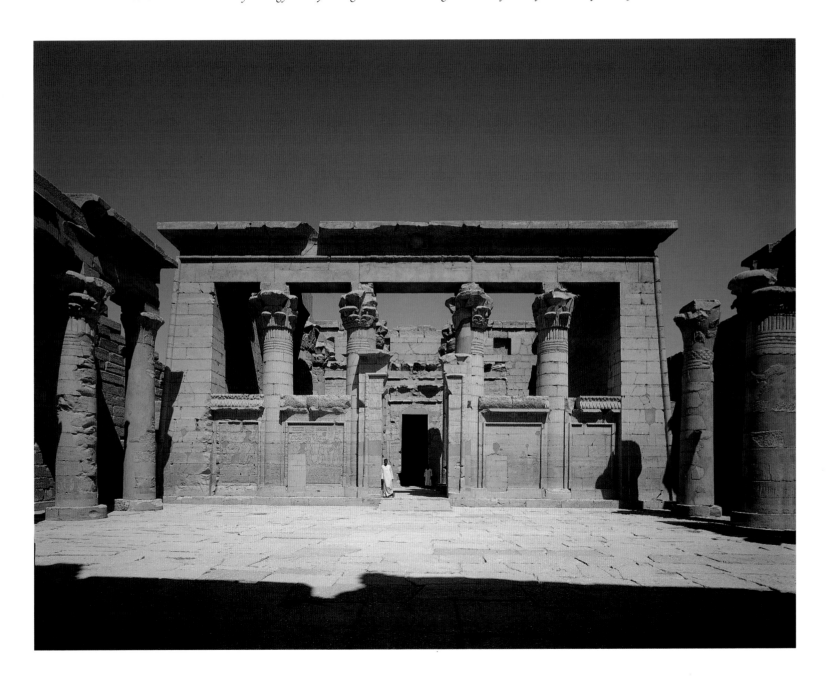

OPPOSITE *The temple of el-Dakka, now at New Sebua, was dedicated to a local form of the god Thoth. Begun by the Meroitic king Arkamani in the late 3rd century BC, it is mostly a Ptolemaic and Roman construction. Here, on the west side of the façade of the PRONAOS, in the upper scene Ptolemy VIII Euergetes II (170–163 and 145–116 BC) offers the land hieroglyph to Osiris and Isis. In the lower scene he is followed by his niece/wife Cleopatra III and two fertility deities.*

ABOVE *This fallen statue of Ramesses II (1279–1213 BC) is one of a pair that originally stood at the entrance to his temple at el-Sebua. The king is portrayed carrying a staff topped with the solar falcon: the temple was dedicated to Ra-Horakhty and Amun-Ra. In the background is the relocated Temple of el-Dakka.*

The Arabic name Wadi el-Sebua means Valley of the Lions and refers to the avenue of sphinxes in front of Ramesses II's temple. It was built under the supervision of Setau, the Viceroy of Kush. The outer parts are free-standing while the sanctuary, transverse hall and hypostyle hall are rock-cut.

Two New Kingdom rock-cut temples have been relocated at New Amada: the temple from the original site, and a temple of Ramesses II (1279–1213 BC) relocated from el-Derr. The rooms of the latter temple were imprecisely hewn and the reliefs are relatively crude in their execution. Nevertheless they still have some vigorous colours.

OPPOSITE   *The Small Temple at New Abu Simbel was dedicated to a local form of Hathor and to Nefertari, the favourite wife of Ramesses II (1279–1213 BC). Four of the 10-metre-high colossi of the façade are of Ramesses II, two of Nefertari. The rock-cut temple extends some 24 metres into the mountain and consists of a hall with six Hathor columns, a transverse hall and a sanctuary.*

BELOW   *The four seated colossi of Ramesses II in the cliff-hewn façade of the Great Temple at New Abu Simbel are over 20 metres in height. Smaller figures of the royal family stand before them. In the upper centre of the façade, figures of Ramesses II (carved in shallow relief) offer images of the goddess Maat, who is holding the User sceptre, to the sun god: this composition is a rebus writing of the prenomen of the pharaoh: User-Maat-Ra.*

OPPOSITE *Eight engaged colossi of an Osiriform Ramesses II stand in the pillared hall of the Great Temple at New Abu Simbel. The sanctuary is visible at the very back.*

ABOVE *In the sanctuary of the Great Temple at New Abu Simbel sit the three major gods of the New Kingdom pantheon and the deified Ramesses II. From left to right are Ptah of Memphis, Amun-Ra of Thebes, the deified Ramesses II and Ra-Horakhty of Heliopolis.*

REBUS: a decorative combination of signs and images that form a picture that can be read hieroglyphically.

SCREEN WALL: a wall made by filling the spaces between the outermost columns of the *pronaos* of a temple to create the façade.

SEASONS: the three seasons of the Egyptian year were the inundation (*akhet*) when the Nile flooded (in the late summer and early autumn); the growing season (*peret*), when seeds planted at the retreat of the flood waters developed and the crops were harvested (up to April); and the drought (*shemu*) leading up to the next appearance of the flood waters.

SED FESTIVAL: the festival of renewal supposedly commemorating the king's thirtieth jubilee (though many kings who are known to have reigned for less than thirty years are depicted celebrating their *sed* festival).

SISTRUM: a musical instrument, usually in the form of a rattle, that was sacred to Hathor.

SPEOS: the Greek word for 'cave', the term is used to describe a rock-cut temple.

STELA: a wooden or stone slab with inscriptions and decorations serving a variety of commemorative, funerary and political functions.

THRONE NAMES: at the coronation the king assumed four names in addition to his birth name (or *nomen*). The *prenomen* usually had the god Ra as the first written component. Both the *nomen* and *prenomen* were written in a cartouche. The 'Horus name' was typically written inside the depiction of the palace façade known as the *serekh* which was surmounted by the falcon god Horus. The 'Golden Horus name' follows a depiction of the falcon above a golden bowl. The 'Two Ladies' or *nebty* name is the name introduced by the cobra goddess Wadjet of Lower Egypt and the vulture goddess Nekhbet of Upper Egypt.

TORUS MOULDING: a decorative, rounded moulding running along the face or edge of a stone wall; it is derived from the binding of wrapped plants used to strengthen mud-brick structures.

FURTHER READING

The books listed below are mostly readily available non-specialist works.

ARCHITECTURE, MONUMENTS, TEMPLES AND TOMBS

David, A.R., 1973. *Religious Ritual at Abydos.* Warminster: Aris and Phillips.

Lehner, M., 1997. *The Complete Pyramids.* London: Thames and Hudson.

Martin, G.T., 1991. *The Hidden Tombs of Memphis.* London: Thames and Hudson.

McDonald, J.K., 1996. *House of Eternity: The Tomb of Nefertari.* London: Thames and Hudson.

Murnane, W.J., 1980. *United with Eternity: a concise guide to the monuments of Medinet Habu.* Chicago: Oriental Institute of the University of Chicago.

Piankoff, A., 1954. *The Tomb of Ramesses VI* (Bollingen Series XL.1., vols 1 and 2). New York: Pantheon.

Quirke, S. (ed.), 1997. *The Temple in Ancient Egypt.* London: British Museum Press.

Reeves, N. and Wilkinson, R.H., 1996. *The Complete Valley of the Kings.* London: Thames and Hudson.

Shafer, B.E. (ed.), 1998. *Temples of Ancient Egypt.* London and New York: I.B. Tauris.

Snape, S., 1996. *Egyptian Temples.* Princes Risborough: Shire.

Strudwick, N. and Strudwick, H., 1999. *Thebes in Egypt: a guide to the tombs and temples of ancient Luxor.* London: British Museum Press.

Watson, P., 1987. *Egyptian Pyramids and Mastaba Tombs.* Princes Risborough: Shire.

Wildung, D, 1997. *Egypt from Prehistory to the Romans.* Cologne: Taschen.

Wilkinson, R.H., 2000. *The Complete Temples of Ancient Egypt.* London: Thames and Hudson.

BIOGRAPHY AND DICTIONARY

Clayton, P.A., 1994. *Chronicle of the Pharaohs.* London: Thames and Hudson.

David, R. and David, A.E., 1992. *A Biographical Dictionary of Ancient Egypt.* London: Seaby.

Kitchen, K.A., 1982. *Pharaoh Triumphant – The Life and Times of Ramesses II.* Cairo: The American University in Cairo Press.

Kozloff, A.E. and Bryan, B.M., 1992. *Egypt's Dazzling Sun – Amenhotep III and his world.* Cleveland: Cleveland Museum of Art.

Redford, D.B., 1984. *Akhenaten the Heretic King.* Princeton: Princeton University Press.

Shaw, I. and Nicholson, P., 1995. *British Museum Dictionary of Ancient Egypt.* London: British Museum Press.

Thomas, A.P., 1988. *Akhenaten's Egypt.* Princes Risborough: Shire.

GEOGRAPHY AND GENERAL OVERVIEW ON SITES

Baines, J. and Málek, J., 2000. *Atlas of Ancient Egypt.* New York: Facts on File.

Manley, B., 1996. *The Penguin Historical Atlas of Ancient Egypt.* London: Penguin.

GUIDE BOOKS

Gohary, J., 1998. *Guide to the Nubian Monuments on Lake Nasser.* Cairo: The American University in Cairo Press.

Haag, M., 1990. *Discovery Guide to Egypt.* London: Michael Haag Ltd.

Hewison, R.N., 1984. *The Fayoum: a practical guide.* Cairo: The American University in Cairo Press.

Kamil, J., 1996. *Luxor.* Cairo: Egypt International Publishing Co.

Kamil, J., 1996. *Sakkara and Memphis.* Cairo: Egypt International Publishing Co.

Kamil, J., 1996. *Upper Egypt and Nubia.* Cairo: Egypt International Publishing Co.

Murnane, W.J., 1983. *The Penguin Guide to Ancient Egypt.* Harmondsworth: Penguin.

Richardson, D. and O'Brien, K., 1991. *Egypt*. London: Rough Guide Ltd.

HIEROGLYPHS AND THE MIDDLE EGYPTIAN LANGUAGE

Collier, M. and Manley, B., 1998. *How to Read Egyptian Hieroglyphs*. London: British Museum Press.

Davies, W.V., 1987. *Egyptian Hieroglyphs*. London: British Museum Press.

Wilkinson, R.H., 1992. *Reading Egyptian Art – A Hieroglyphic Guide to Ancient Egyptian Painting and Sculpture*. London: Thames and Hudson.

ILLUSTRATIONS OF EGYPT FROM THE PAST

Berko, P. and Berko, V. (compilers), 1992. *Ancient Egypt in Nineteenth Century Painting*. Brussels: Berko.

Clayton, P.A., 1982. *The Rediscovery of Ancient Egypt*. London: Thames and Hudson.

Manchip White, J.E., 1980. *Egypt and the Holy Land in Historic Photographs – 77 Views by Francis Frith*. New York: Dover.

Osman, C., 1997. *Egypt Caught in Time*. Cairo: The American University in Cairo Press.

Taschen, B. (publisher), 1994. *Description de l'Égypte*. Cologne. [This is a compressed reprint of: Panckoucke, C.L.F. (publisher), 1809. *Description de l'Égypte ou recueil des observations et des recherches qui ont été faites en Égypte pendant l'expédition de l'armée Française*. Paris: Imperial Press.]

Vaczek L. and Buckland, G., 1981. *Travellers in Ancient Lands – A Portrait of the Middle East, 1839–1919*. Boston: New York Graphic Society.

Vercoutter, J., 1992. *L'Égypte à la Chambre Noire*. Paris: Gallimard.

KINGSHIP, RELIGION AND PHILOSOPHY

Allen, J.P., Assmann, J., Lloyd, A.B., Ritner, R.K. and Silverman, D.P., 1989. *Religion and Philosophy in Ancient Egypt* (Yale Egyptological Studies 3). New Haven: Yale.

Allen, T.G., 1974. *The Book of the Dead or Going Forth by Day* (Studies in Ancient Oriental Civilization no. 37). Chicago: The Oriental Institute of the University of Chicago.

Faulkner, R.O., 1969. *The Ancient Egyptian Pyramid Texts*. Oxford: Oxford University Press.

Frankfort, H., 1948. *Kingship and the Gods – A Study of Ancient Near Eastern Religion as the Integration of Society and Nature*. Chicago: University of Chicago Press.

Hassan, F.A., 1992. 'Primeval goddess to divine king: the mythogenesis of power in the early Egyptian state', in R. Friedman and B. Adams (eds), *The Followers of Horus* (Egyptian Studies Publication 2; Oxbow Monograph 20). Oxford: Oxbow, 307–21.

Hornung, E., 1982. *Conceptions of God in Ancient Egypt* (trans. J. Baines). Ithaca: Cornell University Press.

Hornung, E., 1999. *The Ancient Egyptian Books of the Afterlife* (trans. D. Lorton). Ithaca: Cornell University Press.

Lurker, M., 1980. *The Gods and Symbols of Ancient Egypt* (trans. B. Cummings). London: Thames and Hudson.

Meeks, D. and Favard-Meeks, C., 1997. *Daily Life of the Egyptian Gods* (trans. G.M. Goshgarian). London: John Murray.

Quirke, S., 1992. *Ancient Egyptian Religion*. London: British Museum Press.

Watterson, B., 1996. *Gods of Ancient Egypt*. Stroud: Sutton.

Wilkinson, R.H., 1994. *Symbol and Magic in Egyptian Art*. London: Thames and Hudson.

Witt, R.E., 1971. *Isis in the Graeco-Roman World*. New York: Cornell University Press.

NUBIA

Taylor, J., 1991. *Egypt and Nubia*. London: British Museum Press.

Welsby, D.A., 1996. *The Kingdom of Kush*. London: British Museum Press.

Wildung, D. (ed.) 1997. *Sudan: ancient kingdoms of the Nile*. Paris and New York: Flammarion.

PREHISTORY, UNIFICATION AND HISTORY

Adams, B., 1988. *Predynastic Egypt.* Princes Risborough: Shire.

Bowman, A.K., 1986. *Egypt After the Pharaohs.* London: Guild.

Grimal, N., 1992, *A History of Ancient Egypt* (trans. I. Shaw). Oxford: Blackwell.

Hoffman, M.A., 1980. *Egypt Before the Pharaohs.* London: Routledge and Kegan Paul.

James, T.G.H., 1979. *An Introduction to Ancient Egypt.* London: British Museum Press.

Kemp, B.J., 1989. *Ancient Egypt: Anatomy of a Civilization.* London: Routledge.

Redford, D.B., 1992. *Egypt, Canaan, and Israel in Ancient Times.* Princeton: Princeton University Press.

Shaw, I. (ed.), 2000. *The Oxford History of Ancient Egypt.* Oxford: Oxford University Press.

Spencer, A.J., 1993. *Early Egypt: the rise of civilization in the Nile Valley.* London: British Museum Press.

Trigger, B.G., Kemp, B.J., O'Connor, D. and Lloyd, A.B., 1983. *Ancient Egypt A Social History.* Cambridge: Cambridge University Press.

RECENT DISCOVERIES

Davies, V. and Friedman, R., 1998. *Egypt.* London: British Museum Press.